There's no limit to the number of foods—fresh, canned and frozen—that are tempting and delicious when cooked in casseroles. Meats become tender and juicy, vegetables take on new and savory tastes, leftovers become festive.

In this book **James Beard** gives you a great variety of his favorite casserole recipes, and he makes them easy to follow. And once you try these casseroles, you'll realize that oven cooking is one of the finest ways of preparing food for any occasion—as well as being easy and inexpensive.

JAMES BEARD'S
CASSEROLE
COOKBOOK

FAWCETT GOLD MEDAL • NEW YORK

JAMES BEARD'S CASSEROLE COOKBOOK

Published by Fawcett Gold Medal Books, a unit of CBS Publications, the Consumer Publishing Division of CBS Inc., by arrangement with Maco Publishing Co., Inc., New York, New York.

Printed in the United States of America

First Fawcett Gold Medal printing: December 1972

Contents

JAMES BEARD'S
CASSEROLE
COOKBOOK

ALL ABOUT CASSEROLES

Here's the easy, foolproof—and
inexpensive—way to serve great meals

Like many of the tastiest dishes served in America
today, the casserole is an ingenious European idea with
a unique American twist. It all began in France where
peasant families—who regard a good meal and a good
bank account with almost equal reverence—discovered
that inexpensive odds and ends of food acquired an almost miraculous savor when oven-cooked slowly in
earthenware pots.

Then American chefs took over and discovered that
the French had found out only one of the benefits of
this enormously practical dish. There are others:

Because it can hold an entire meal in one container,
it's a godsend to beginning cooks, harried housewives
and the millions of apartment-dwellers who are ham-
pered by tiny modern kitchens and inadequate and
cramped serving space.

It's perfect for company dinners because the dish
can be prepared in advance and, in most instances, will
not suffer if left in the oven until guests straggle into
the dining room.

It's an ideal work saver because it can be whisked
right from the oven to the table and its contents dished
out piping hot onto the dinner plates.

The casserole is a decorative oven-to-table dish.

A particularly beautiful pottery casserole can serve as a magnificent centerpiece to a delightful buffet supper or patio dinner party.

And, what's more, not only can a casserole give you a delicious meal out of odds and ends, it can provide a variety of ways to cook the fine foods available to the average American housewife.

Casserole cooking includes a much wider variety of foods than most people realize. Any food that is normally braised, stewed, baked or sautéed can be oven-prepared. In fact, many foods gain by it. A beef pot roast, for example, if tightly covered and cooked slowly in a low oven, will be tender, juicy and flavorful.

Most cereals—rice, corn, cracked wheat, barley and other grain foods—are greatly improved by oven cooking. Rice baked in broth is far tastier than rice boiled or steamed over direct heat. Many rich soups, if cooked slowly in the oven, mellow and blend more thoroughly. Vegetables change their taste and sometimes even their texture in oven cooking, giving added variety to the menu. Many simple fruit desserts become gourmet's delights if baked with a wine or liqueur sauce.

Finally, and most important, the casserole method tends to stimulate a creative interest in cooking. If the cook has even the least amount of imagination, he or she will soon begin to experiment and to invent new twists—adding to the recipe or making up an entirely new combination. At this point, cooking becomes an art and the cook a true artist. (See Chapter 10 for help in improvising.)

some do's and don't's

DO select a casserole that will accommodate your food. A small amount of food at the bottom of a huge container looks awful, but it's even worse to pack a small dish too full. It will probably spill over the side in the oven, making an unattractive dish to bring to the table.

DON'T try to rush foods that are oven-cooked. They will be tender and tasty only if they are cooked slowly.

DO place a pan under the casserole in the oven to catch any overflow of liquid. It's easier to clean a pan than an oven.

DON'T add cold liquids to a hot casserole. Heat the liquids first. Cold liquids slow the cooking process and may crack the casserole if it is of breakable material. This can be a real catastrophe.

DO weight meat loaves and pâtés while they cool by covering them with a piece of aluminum foil and balancing a heavy item on top. Tins of canned food or an electric iron will do. This improves the texture.

DON'T trust to luck. Taste before you serve.

DO serve soufflés and egg dishes the moment they are ready. They bear no waiting.

DON'T serve the same casserole to the same guests twice in a row. If you entertain a lot, keep a record.

DO transfer leftovers to another dish for storage.

DON'T put a hot casserole in the refrigerator or in an iced container. Let it cool to room temperature first.

DO have plenty of thick pot holders. Casseroles are heavy and hot.

DON'T overcook. This is the fault of most beginners.

DO reduce the oven temperature if the meal is delayed. Check the liquid to make sure the dish won't dry out.

DON'T add too much liquid to the food. It is better to add a little more during the cooking process than to have the final result watery.

how to use this book

You will find in Chapters 2-9 a handsome variety of casserole dishes in a number of categories. By judicious selection, the cook can serve delicious and exciting meals on all occasions, whether a simple supper for the family or a large party for important guests.

Personally, I am not a believer in one-dish meals. I find them too monotonous. It seems to me that at least a salad should be added. Contrasts in texture, flavor and appearance are important features in any appetizing meal. If your main dish is a casserole that is rich and flavorful, then complement it with a crisp vegetable. It may be something raw in a fresh-tasting dunk sauce or a green vegetable cooked to the bitey stage and dressed simply with a dab of butter and perhaps a dash of lemon juice. You'll find these suggestions with the individual recipes and, in Chapter 11, a whole section on accompaniments.

A casserole need not always be the main dish, but can be the side dish that makes the dinner. If you're preparing a simple roast, look through Chapter 7 for a flavorful vegetable casserole such as rice baked in

Pyrex ovenware with Pennsylvania Dutch motif.

broth. On the other hand, a rich vegetable casserole should be accompanied by something unadorned, such as a grilled chop.

If the main course is heavy, select a refreshing dessert—baked pears, or fresh fruit with a dash of liqueur. But if you are planning a simple light luncheon of salad, look for a dessert recipe that is richer, something like a chocolate soufflé. If your main dish has a heavy sauce, or quite a bit of liquid, you won't want to serve sauces on the vegetables or on the dessert.

In general, when you plan your menu use your own common sense in combining foods that taste good together.

A word of warning: When planning your meal, take into account what utensils you have and the space available for cooking.

2

MEATS

Casserole cooking is an
exciting way to serve
almost any cut of meat, even
the most inexpensive

I'll concede that of all the meats available to the average American male, steak is probably the favorite. Yet there are many other flavorful cuts of beef and many other meats that ought to be considered, if only for the sake of variety—and of your pocketbook. And there are always leftovers. Most meats, even the cheapest and toughest, respond to long, slow cooking in a tightly covered casserole, and become tasty and tender. Actually, many classic meat dishes are cooked by this method, and for good reason. The proper combination of meat, herbs, seasonings, juices and perhaps a touch of wine, gently cooked together for hours, develops a rich and mellow flavor found in no broiled steak.

Here are recipes that are good "as is" and also good for experimenting. Try your own ideas in herbs and seasonings—you'll find that using your imagination is the way to cooking success, and to fun as well.

---

an old favorite
RANCH CASSEROLE

Have 2½ pounds of **Beef Chuck** or **Round Steak** cut in 2-inch chunks. Dredge these in **Flour** seasoned with **Salt** and **Pepper,** and brown them quickly in 3 tablespoons of **Bacon Fat** or **Butter.** Transfer them to a casserole and add 2 crushed cloves of **Garlic,** 1 large **Onion** stuck with 3 **Cloves,** 1 teaspoon of **Thyme** or **Oregano** and 1 cup of **Water.** Cover the casserole and place in a 350°F. oven for 1½ hours.

Meanwhile, parboil 6 young **Carrots** until almost tender. Reserve the liquid. Drain the liquid from 1 jar or tin of small **White Onions** and combine the onion liquid with the carrot liquid. To this add 2 **Bouillon Cubes.** Bring it to a boil and boil for 10 minutes. Knead 3 tablespoons of **Butter** with 2 tablespoons of flour, using a fork or your fingers. Sprinkle the balls of butter and flour over the surface of the cooking liquid and stir thoroughly until smooth and thickened.

Add this thickened liquid to the casserole and also add the carrots and onions. Continue cooking in the oven until tender and thoroughly blended. Just before serving, remove the cover and top with a border of **Mashed Potatoes.** In the center, heap frozen **Green Peas** cooked according to directions on the package. When completed, it will look extraordinarily tempting and delicious. Serves 6 to 8.

a quick version
MEAT BALLS AND MACARONI

This is a simple approach to a famous recipe that takes days of preparation. Heat 2 tablespoons of **Olive** or **Peanut Oil** and add 1½ cups of finely chopped **Onions,** 1 finely chopped **Green Pepper** and 1 cup of **Sliced Mushrooms.** Cook them together for 7 to 8 minutes. Add 1 cup of **Canned Tomatoes** (the Italian plum variety are best) and let this simmer while you prepare the meat. Season 1 pound of **Chopped Beef** with **Salt** and **Pepper** and a bit of **Basil,** and form it into tiny meat balls. Brown these in 2 tablespoons of butter, rolling the pan around to be sure the meat is browned on all sides.

In the bottom of a casserole, arrange a layer of cooked **Noodles, Spaghetti** or **Macaroni** and cover with half of the meat balls. Add another layer of the pasta, then the rest of the meat balls. Finally top with a third layer of pasta and pour the sauce over all. Sprinkle with grated cheese, cover and bake at 375° F. for 30 minutes. Cook with the cover removed for the last 10 minutes and then add a little more cheese. Serves 4.

Serve this with a salad of tomatoes and romaine tossed with a good garlicky dressing. Bread and cheese complete this dinner to perfection.

real eye opener
CORNED BEEF HASH IN CASSEROLE

Pack 2 cans of **Corned Beef Hash** into a buttered casserole. Dot with **Butter.** Bake the hash at 350° F. until nicely browned on top—about 20 to 30 minutes. Serves 4 to 6.

Serve the hash in the casserole with a side dish of scrambled eggs mixed with plenty of chopped parsley.

Or, if you want something different in the hash line, hard-boil 6 **Eggs.** Chop the whites and mash the yolks. Chop coarsely one 2-pound can of **Corned Beef.** Melt 4 tablespoons of **Butter** in a skillet and sauté 2 large **Onions,** chopped with 2 cloves of **Garlic.** Add 1 tablespoon of **Worcestershire Sauce** (or add 1 teaspoon **Curry Powder** mixed with 1 tablespoon **Water)** and then mashed egg yolks. Blend and toss together lightly with the chopped egg whites and the corned beef. Place beef mixture in a greased casserole, sprinkle the top with buttered **Crumbs** and bake at 400° F. for 20 minutes.

Either one of these is a good breakfast or brunch dish. Have a platter of sliced tomatoes, hot buttered corn muffins, comb honey—and coffee, of course.

great hot or cold
GOOD HONEST MEAT LOAF

Combine 1 pound each of ground **Beef, Pork** and **Veal** with ½ cup each of chopped green **Onions** and **Parsley,** 1 teaspoon **Salt,** 1½ teaspoons freshly ground **Pepper,** 2 beaten **Eggs,** ½ cup fresh **Bread Crumbs** which have been soaked in **Bouillon,** ½ teaspoon **Rosemary** and a pinch of **Nutmeg.** Mix thoroughly with the hands. Shape into a loaf and place on a layer of **Bacon Strips, Pork Skins** or **Salt Pork Strips** in an earthenware baking dish or casserole. Top with a few strips of bacon or salt pork and bake uncovered at 325° F. for 1½ to 2 hours. This is grand hot, but much better—to my taste buds—weighted down and served cold. Serves 6 to 8.

Variations

1. With Vegetables (Bouquetière): Prepare as above. Place in large casserole or baking dish, top with **Carrot** strips, and surround with whole **Baby Carrots** and small **White Onions.** Bake at 325° F. for 45 minutes. Add small whole **Potatoes** and small whole **Turnips** which have been parboiled for 10 minutes. Baste with pan juices and continue baking 45 minutes longer, until meat is thoroughly done.

2. Italian: Add 3 cloves finely chopped **Garlic,** 1 cup whole, pitted **Ripe Olives,** ½ cup **Tomato Pureé** and 1

teaspoon fresh **Basil** instead of the rosemary to the meat mixture. Cover the loaf with a thin layer of tomato pureé and top with **Bacon** or **Salt Pork Strips.** Cook as above.

3. French: Combine 1 pound **Pork,** 1 pound **Veal** and 1 pound chopped **Liver** with the seasonings given in the basic recipe. Add 1 cup **Red Wine** to the pan and baste with the wine and the pan juices frequently.

4. California: Add 2 chopped cloves **Garlic** and 1 cup pimento-stuffed **Olives** to the basic loaf. Add ½ cup **Orange Juice** and the juice of 2 **Lemons** to the pan and baste frequently.

5. Northwest: Add 1 7-ounce can of minced **Clams** with their juice to the mixture and proceed as above.

6. Indian: Add 2 cloves of **Garlic,** finely chopped, 2 chopped **Green Peppers,** ½ cup **Tomato Pureé** and 1½ tablespoons **Curry Powder** to the basic mixture; baste with 1 cup **Pineapple Juice** mixed with 1 teaspoon curry powder. Serve with chopped **Almonds, Chutney** and a **Curry Sauce** (see next recipe), French-fried **Onions** and **Rice Pilaff.**

7. Mexican: Add 1 tablespoon **Chili Powder,** 1 pinch fresh **Cumin,** ½ cup **Pine Nuts** and 3 small **Green Peppers,** finely chopped, to the basic mixture. Baste with a combination of ½ cup **Tomato Puree,** ½ cup **Tomato Juice,** 3 finely chopped cloves of **Garlic** and 1 tablespoon **Chili Powder.**

Hot, these loaves are elegant with rice or mashed potatoes or with crisped fried ones. Broiled or baked tomatoes should go along too. Cold, they should have a rice salad or a potato salad and perhaps hot asparagus with Hollandaise sauce. Try melon for dessert.

CURRY SAUCE

Heat 6 tablespoons of **Butter** in a skillet and sauté 2 finely chopped medium **Onions,** 2 finely chopped cloves of **Garlic,** 2 finely chopped **Carrots,** 2 soaked and seeded **Chili Peppers** and 2 finely chopped unpeeled **Apples.** Cover the pan and simmer for 15 minutes. Add 2 cups of **Consomme** or **Chicken Broth** and re-cover the pan. Simmer for 45 minutes.

Add 1 or 2 tablespoons of **Curry Powder,** according to your taste, 1 teaspoon of **Salt,** a little grated fresh **Ginger** or chopped preserved ginger, and ½ cup of **Coconut Milk.** (If this is not available, soak 1 cup of grated coconut in 1 cup of cream for 1 hour. Squeeze all the liquid out of the coconut and add it to the sauce.)

Bring the sauce to a boil, taste for seasoning and serve with any meat, fish or vegetable that you like in a curry dish.

omnibus dish
BEEF AND VEGETABLE LOAF

Combine 2 pounds finely ground **Beef** with ½ pound ground **Salt Pork,** ½ cup soft **Bread Crumbs,** 1 finely grated large **Onion,** 1 finely grated large **Carrot,** 1 finely grated **Green Pepper,** 2 cloves finely chopped **Garlic,** ½ cup chopped **Green Onion,** ½ cup chopped **Parsley,** 3 beaten **Eggs,** 1 teaspoon **Salt,** 1 teaspoon **Dry Mustard,** and 2 tablespoons **Chili Sauce.**

Form into a loaf when blended well together and place on **Bacon** strips in a casserole. Top with onion rings and thinly sliced carrot. Add more strips of bacon or salt pork, bake, covered, 1 hour at 325° F. Uncover and continue baking for 35 to 45 minutes, basting frequently. Serves 4 to 6.

This is amazingly good with marble-sized potatoes browned in butter until crisp. Serve with them a romaine salad with a lemon-juice, olive-oil dressing. Have a good pumpkin pie for dessert.

real man's dish!
BEEFSTEAK IN CASSEROLE

Buy a 2-inch-thick cut of **Round Steak** weighing about 3 pounds. Sprinkle it with 1 cup of **Flour,** lay it on a board or solid table and pound the flour into the meat with the edge of a sturdy plate.

Brown the steak quickly on both sides in **Bacon Fat** and remove it to a casserole. Brown 1 sliced **Onion** in the remaining fat and add that to the meat. Pour on 1 cup **Red Wine** or **Stock** and add 1 **Bay Leaf** and a sprig of **Thyme.** Cover and bake 2 hours at 325° F. **Potatoes** and **Carrots** may be added to the casserole for the last hour of cooking; or **Mushroom** caps or sliced mushrooms for the last 30 minutes. Serves 4.

after a steak
QUICK BEEFSTEAK PIE

Dice 2 cups leftover **Beef.** Sauté 2 medium **Onions** in 3 tablespoons **Butter** until just soft. Combine with the beef, season with ½ teaspoon **Salt,** ½ cup **Chili Sauce,** 1 can **Beef Gravy** and ½ pound sautéed sliced **Mushrooms** (optional). Blend well with beef, spoon into a casserole and top with **Biscuit Mix,** which you have mixed according to directions on the package, having added ⅓ cup chopped **Parsley.** Bake at 425° F. for 15 minutes and reduce to 350° F. for 5 to 6 minutes more.

Serve with cole slaw, garlic toast and, for dessert, frozen raspberries and peaches.

England's finest
BEEFSTEAK AND KIDNEY PIE

Cut 3 pounds of **Round Steak** or **Rump Steak** into strips 3 inches long and about 1 inch wide. Dredge with **Seasoned Flour** and brown very quickly in hot **Beef Fat.**

Beefsteak and kidney pie is an English classic.

Skin, clean and slice thin 8 **Lamb's Kidneys.** When the kidneys are almost tender, brown them quickly in 3 tablespoons **Butter.** Do not let them cook after the browning.

Now arrange beef strips and sliced kidneys in alternate layers in a 2-quart casserole. Pour in the liquid from the cooked beef, adding more stock if necessary to bring it to 1 inch below the top of the casserole. It is a good idea to place a jelly glass or custard cup in the center of the casserole to hold up the crust.

Now prepare a rich **Pastry Dough** and cover the casserole with it, pressing the edges down firmly. Make several gashes in it to allow the steam to escape and brush it with lightly beaten **Egg Yolk.**

Add ¼ teaspoon **Thyme,** 1 large **Onion,** chopped fine, and enough **Stock** or **Water** to just barely cover the meat. Simmer 1 to 1½ hours.

Place in a very hot oven at 450° F. and bake for 10 minutes. Reduce the temperature to 350° F. and bake until the crust is nicely browned—about 30 minutes. Serves 4 to 6.

Serve this English classic with boiled potatoes and parsley butter, plus a salad. For dessert, crisp fresh apples with a sharp cheddar cheese. A bottle of ice-cold beer or ale really rounds this meal off.

sticks to your ribs
BEEF KIDNEY CASSEROLE

Soak 2 **Beef Kidneys** in lightly salted water for 3 hours. Drain and slice into small pieces. Place a layer of the sliced kidneys in a casserole. Spread a layer of thinly sliced **Potatoes** over the kidneys. Sprinkle with **Salt, Pepper** and **Thyme.** Repeat these layers, ending up with a layer of potatoes and seasonings. Pour over all a can of **Beef Gravy** and bake at 325° F. for 45 minutes. Serves 4 to 6.

variations on a classic
POT ROAST

Have your butcher lard well a piece of **Beef** weighing 4 to 6 pounds. Dredge it in **Seasoned Flour** and brown it quickly on all sides in 4 tablespoons of **Fat.** Place it in a deep casserole with the remaining fat and 1 cup of **Stock, Wine** or **Water.** Cover tightly and cook in the oven at 325° F. about 2 hours or until thoroughly tender. Allow 25 minutes for each pound. Add more liquid if necessary. Serves 6 to 8.

This is excellent with boiled potatoes, glazed onions and an assortment of pickles. Try a blueberry puff for dessert.
Variations
   1. Italian Style: Stud the meat with thin slivers of

Garlic, allowing 2 good-sized cloves for a 5-pound piece of beef. Brown quickly in **Olive Oil** and remove to casserole. Add 2 large sliced **Onions,** 1 **Bay Leaf,** ½ teaspoon **Thyme,** 1 teaspoon **Salt,** 1 teaspoon **Pepper,** 1 tablespoon chopped **Parsley,** ½ cup **Tomato Pureé** and ½ cup **Stock.** Cook as above. Before serving, skim any excess fat from the pan juices and stir in an additional cup of the tomato purée.

Serve with buttered noodles, buttered fresh asparagus and sliced tomatoes. For an extra-special touch, try some pears in red wine for dessert.

2. With Wine: Wipe the roast with a damp cloth and season with **Salt** and **Pepper.** Lard the meat well with ¼-inch strips of **Salt Pork.** Brown it on all sides and place it in the casserole. Pour on 6 tablespoons of **Cognac** and blaze. Extinguish the flame and add 1 clove **Garlic,** 1 **Bay Leaf,** a pinch of **Thyme** and 2 cups red or white **Wine.** Cook as above.

About 45 minutes before the meat is done, add 12 small **White Onions** and 4 or 5 scraped and quartered **Carrots** to the casserole; also more wine if necessary. When tender, skim any excess fat from the pan drippings to serve with the roast.

This is good with either mashed potatoes or buttered noodles. Try a salad of Boston lettuce, ripe olives and sliced hard-boiled eggs with a mayonnaise thinned with buttermilk.

for hearty eaters

RUMP POT ROAST

Select a 5-pound piece of **Rump** and have it wrapped with fat. Peel 4 cloves **Garlic** and insert them into the roast with the aid of a sharply pointed knife. Sprinkle with 1 full teaspoon **Rosemary** and place in a large casserole with 3 **Carrots,** 2 **Leeks** and 3 **Onions.** Sprinkle with **Salt** and **Pepper** and sear at 500° F. for 30 minutes. Add ½ cup **Red Wine** or **Consommé** and cover tightly. Reduce the heat to 300° F. and continue cooking for 2½ hours. Again reduce the heat to 200° F. and cook until proper degree of tenderness has been achieved.

Pour off the juices of the pan and plunge the container into ice water so that the fat comes to the top. Remove fat and add 1 can **Beef Gravy** to the juices and a dash of freshly chopped **Onion** and **Parsley.** Heat to boiling point, add ½ cup **Heavy Cream** and correct the seasoning. Serves 8 to 10.

old-country style
HUNGARIAN POT ROAST

Have a butcher lard a 4- to 6-pound **Pot Roast** with ¼-inch strips of **Salt Pork.** Sear it well in 4 tablespoons of **Butter** or **Olive Oil.** Place in a casserole with 1 teaspoon **Salt,** 1½ teaspoons **Hungarian Paprika,** ¼ teaspoon **Nutmeg** and ½ cup **Stock.** Cover and cook 25 minutes to the pound at 325°F., adding more liquid if needed. When done, skim excess fat from sauce. Add another teaspoon of paprika and 1 cup of thick **Sour Cream.** Blend thoroughly. Serves 6 to 8.

Buttered noodles generously sprinkled with parsley are a must with this, as are sautéed mushrooms. And this might be a good time for an easy dessert that you'll never forget—make a pile of thin, thin pancakes. Put scrapings of sweet chocolate between each one as you pile them up; cut in edges, like cake, and serve with whipped cream.

from the range
TEXAS CASSEROLE BEEF

Dredge 2 pounds of thinly sliced **Beef Round** with **Flour** and season with **Salt** and **Pepper.** Sear very quickly in **Beef Fat** or **Butter** and remove to a casserole which has a layer of **Bacon** in the bottom. Add 1 thinly sliced **Onion,** 2 finely chopped **Garlic** cloves, 1 cup **Tomato Sauce** into which you have stirred 2 tablespoons **Chili Powder,** 1 teaspoon **Salt,** 1 teaspoon **Black Pepper.** Cover with 1 large can **Kidney Beans** and dot with a little butter. Cover and bake at 350° F. for 1 hour, or until the beef is tender.

Serve with rice (the instant variety is fast and sure), crisp radishes and carrot sticks. For dessert, try strawberries with orange juice.

exotic touch

BEEF CASSEROLE WITH OLIVES

Peel 12 small **White Onions** and brown them very lightly in 3 tablespoons **Beef Fat** or **Butter.** Next, take 2½ pounds **Chuck Beef**—cut in good-sized cubes and dredged well in **Flour** seasoned with **Salt** and freshly ground **Black Pepper.** Brown quickly and place with the onions in a casserole. Add ½ teaspoon freshly ground black pepper and 1 teaspoon **Rosemary.** Pour over the meat 1 cup **Stock** or **Bouillon,** cover and bake 1 hour at 350° F. Remove cover and add 1 cup **Green Olives** (the small Italian or Spanish are the best for this) and ¼ cup chopped **Parsley.** Re-cover and continue cooking at the same temperature for another 30 minutes or until the meat is tender. Serves 4 to 6.

Variations

1. Nicoise: Substitute 1 cup **Tomato Purée** and ½ cup **Tomato Juice** for the stock. Add 2 cloves **Garlic,** minced, and substitute **Ripe Olives** for the green.

2. Belgian: Substitute 1 cup **Beer** for the stock and top the meat with a generous layer of sliced **Onion.**

This dish and its variations really call for liquid accompaniment. Either a good red wine or a bottle of beer is delicious! And for the meal itself, serve the meat with braised cabbage, boiled small new potatoes and a selection of pickles.

a hearty change

BOEUF EN DAUBE AU VIN BLANC

Chop finely 1 large **Onion**, 1 large **Carrot** and ½ pound **Smoked Ham.** Spread these evenly over the bottom of a deep casserole. Place on these a 3-pound **Roast of Round**—top or bottom—and 1 **Calf's Foot.** Add 3 cups **White Wine**, 1 cup **Water** and 1 cup **Stock.** Cover and cook in a very slow oven (250° to 275° F.) 3 hours. Turn the meat; add more liquid in the original proportion, to bring the amount in the casserole to about 4 cups. Season with **Salt** to taste, 1 **Bay Leaf** and a few **Peppercorns.** Cover and cook 3 hours longer.

Remove meat and strain and reserve the stock. There should be several cups. Return the meat to the casserole and set it aside. When the stock cools, skim off any fat; pour the clear liquid back over the meat and let it chill. Serve the meat cold in its own jelly.

As the whole object of this dish is to have the clear jelly around the meat, the deeper and narrower your casserole is, the better the final results will be. Serves 6 to 8.

for adventurers

BOEUF À L'AIL

Have your butcher cut 2 pounds of **Round Steak** into cubes about 1 inch square. Place these in a mixing bowl with 1½ cups **Soy Sauce**, 2 crushed cloves of **Garlic** and 1 tablespoon of **Lemon Juice.** Let stand for 3 hours. Drain the meat, reserving the marinade, and brown it quickly in **Butter.** Transfer to a casserole.

Add 2 minced cloves **Garlic**, 1 large **Onion**, thickly sliced, and 2 **Carrots**, thinly sliced. Sprinkle all lightly with **Flour**, dot with **Butter** and add a grating of **Fresh Ginger.** Cover with a layer of peeled, sliced **Tomatoes.** Pour on ½ cup **Red Wine** or **Stock** and ¼ cup of the strained marinade. Cover and bake 2 hours at 300° F., adding more wine or stock if needed.

Chop coarsely 24 **Chestnuts** which have been roasted and peeled. Sauté them lightly in butter. Then add ¼ cup of the marinade and 1 cup chopped **Mushrooms.** Simmer for 3 minutes.

At the end of 2 hours, spread this mixture over the casserole. Cook uncovered 20 minutes more. Serves 6.

As long as it's a casserole dinner, you might serve this with a barley casserole and perhaps a grapefruit and avocado salad. A good cheese would be a splendid addition; and serve baked apples with chopped nuts for dessert.

ever try tripe?

TRIPES À LA NICOISE

Peel and slice 4 medium-sized **Onions.** Peel and seed 1 pound of **Tomatoes.** Heat ¼ cup **Olive Oil** in a deep earthenware casserole and sauté the onions lightly; then add the tomatoes, ½ teaspoon **Thyme,** ½ teaspoon **Rosemary** and **Salt** and **Pepper** to taste. Simmer till well blended.

Add 1 pint **Vin Rosé.** Stir till smooth. Then add 1 **Calf's Foot** split in half and 2 pounds of **Tripe** cut into neat strips about 1 by 3 inches. Mix well with the tomato sauce. Cover and bake for 3 hours at 325° F. Correct the seasoning and sprinkle liberally with grated **Parmesan Cheese.**

This dish is really better served the next day. If made to be leftover, do not add the grated cheese until it's reheated for the table. Serves 4 to 6.

Boiled or fluffy baked potatoes always seem necessary with tripe, as does French bread. Somehow it also always needs the crispness of a green salad.

French masterpiece

BRAISED BEEF BOURGEOISE

Lard well 5 pounds of rolled boned **Chuck Beef** with strips of **Bacon.** Rub the meat well with **Salt, Pepper** and **Nutmeg.** Place it in a good-sized bowl and pour in 2 cups of **Red Wine** and ½ cup of **Brandy.** Let it marinate 6 hours, turning it occasionally.

Then place the beef in a heavy pot with the marinade. Simmer it gently 1¾ hours with 2 small **Calf's Feet.** Remove the beef to a casserole. Cut the meat from the calf's feet and add to the beef. Add 4 sliced **Carrots,** 12 medium **Onions** and 6 white **Turnips,** cut in half and glazed in **Butter.** Strain the liquid in which the meat was cooked over the meat and bake at 325° F. for 45 minutes. Add more wine if necessary. Serve hot or let jell and serve cold. Serves 6 to 8.

veal

substantial dish
VEAL AND NOODLES

Cook 1 pound **Noodles** in boiling salted water about 9 minutes until tender, not mushy. Peel 1 pound small **White Onions** and boil until tender in 1 can of condensed **Chicken Broth** and an equal amount of **White Wine.** Skim out onions, reserving broth.

Dredge well 3 pounds of **Veal,** sliced very thin, in **Flour** seasoned with **Dry Mustard, Thyme, Marjoram, Salt** and **Pepper.** Brown the veal well in **Fat** in a skillet. When browned and drained on absorbent paper, sprinkle each slice with grated **Lemon Rind.** Cook 1 package of **Frozen Peas,** according to instructions.

In a large, shallow casserole place layers of the veal, noodles, onions and peas.

Melt 6 tablespoons of **Butter** in top of a double-boiler, blend in 6 tablespoons of flour; add 2 cups of **Milk** and 2 cups of the onion broth. Stir constantly until creamy smooth. Salt and pepper to taste. Pour this mixture over the layers in casserole and bake at

Veal with noodles is a rich dish, elegant enough to serve to guests.

375° F. until bubbly—about 45 minutes. Garnish with sliced, pitted **Ripe Olives,** or add these before baking. Serves 8.

For a nice addition, serve a delicately herbed beet and egg salad with onion rings and melba toast. Some chilled fruit would make an excellent dessert.

meal in itself

VEAL STEW WITH VEGETABLES

Have your butcher cut the meat from a 3-pound **Shank of Veal** into good-sized cubes. Cook the bone, cracked, in 4 cups **Water** with 1 medium **Onion** (sliced or quartered), 10 **Peppercorns,** 2 teaspoons **Salt,** ¼ teaspoon **Celery Salt** and 1 **Bay Leaf.** Simmer, covered, for 1¼ hours.

Dredge the meat in **Seasoned Flour** and brown it well in **Butter** or **Olive Oil**. Remove to a casserole. In the remaining fat, sauté lightly 1 cup diced raw **Carrots** and 2 cups peeled, chopped **Tomato**. Add to the meat with the strained broth. Cover and cook 40 minutes at 350° F.

Add 2 cups diced **Potatoes** and salt and **Pepper** to taste. Cover and cook 30 minutes longer. When the vegetables are tender, stir in 1 tablespoon each chopped **Parsley** and **Chives**. Sprinkle generously with grated **Parmesan Cheese** just before serving. Serves 4.

This casserole needs only a tossed green salad and some crisp, hot Italian bread.

one-dish banquet
VEAL SCALLOPS IN CASSEROLE

The amounts to be used in this recipe are largely a matter of choice, but for 4 people you will need about 1½ pounds of **Veal Scallops** which your butcher will cut for you. You will also need 2 medium-sized sliced **Onions**, 3 or 4 **Tomatoes**, peeled and sliced, 4 to 6 **Carrots**, scraped and sliced very thin, ½ to ¾ pound of sliced fresh **Mushrooms** and ½ cup of **Ripe Olives**, pitted and either sliced or whole.

Arrange the veal and the vegetables in alternate layers in a buttered casserole, seasoning each with **Salt** and freshly ground **Black Pepper**. Dot generously with **Butter** and pour on ½ cup **Red Wine** or **Stock**. Cover and bake 1 hour at 300°F.

Add a layer of thinly sliced **Potatoes**. Sprinkle with seasonings and brush well with butter. Increase the oven heat to 350° F. and cook uncovered 35 to 45 minutes or till the potatoes are cooked through and crusted.

You'll need nothing with this but a salad—perhaps endive and celery—and crisp French bread. For dessert try lemon sherbet made from a mix.

Veal surprise includes mushrooms, onions, olives and sliced sausage, baked together in a tomato and consommé sauce redolent with herbs.

---

savory and flavory

VEAL SURPRISE

Cut 2 pounds of **Veal Shoulder** or **Leg** into 2-inch cubes. Dredge well with **Flour** and brown quickly in 2 tablespoons **Butter** and ¼ cup **Olive Oil** with 1 crushed clove of **Garlic.** Place in a deep casserole and add 1 cup **Tomato Purée,** 1 pint **Consommé,** ½ **Bay Leaf,** ¼ teaspoon **Thyme,** ½ teaspoon **Marjoram** and **Salt** and freshly ground **Black Pepper** to taste. Bake 1 hour at 350° F.

Add 12 small **White Onions** lightly sautéed in butter, ¼ pound sliced fresh **Mushrooms,** 1 cup pitted **Ripe Olives** (sliced or whole), 1 teaspoon **Chili Powder** and 2 **Chorizos** (Spanish sausages) cut in slices. Bake 30 minutes longer and rectify the seasoning. Serves 4 to 6.

Serve with fluffy rice, endive and celery stalks and hot rolls. For dessert, try fresh pineapple.

tender and juicy

VEAL ROAST IN CASSEROLE

Have your butcher lard a 4- to 5-pound **Rump Roast of Veal.** Dredge it well in **Seasoned Flour** and brown it quickly in **Butter.** Place it in a deep casserole with 1 **Bay Leaf,** ¼ teaspoon **Thyme,** ½ clove minced **Garlic** and a scraped and quartered **Carrot.** Add 2 cups **Water** and 2 tablespoons **Butter.** Cover and cook 1 hour at 300° F., basting frequently. Uncover and remove carrot and bay leaf. Add 16 to 20 small **White Onions** and more water if necessary. Cook another 30 minutes longer and add 16 to 20 medium-sized **Mushroom Caps.** Cook half an hour longer, uncovered, until meat is tender. Stir ½ cup **Sour Cream** and 1 tablespoon chopped **Chives** into the pan juices and serve. Serves 4 to 6.

Noodles and an endive salad are excellent with this particular veal dish. For dessert, make a white cake and serve it with sliced bananas and whipped cream.

something of interest

CALF'S HEART

Wash and trim 1 **Calf's Heart** carefully. Slit open, wash again and fill with a dressing made of 2 cups **Bread Crumbs,** 1 finely chopped medium **Onion,** 3 tablespoons **Bacon Drippings,** ½ teaspoon ground **Ginger, Salt** and **Pepper** to taste.

Tie heart firmly back in place with string. Dredge it in **Flour** and brown it quickly in a skillet in more bacon drippings. Place in a casserole with 2 cups **Stock** (1 cup of **Red Wine** may be substituted for 1 cup of stock). Cover and bake for 2½ to 3 hours at 350°F., basting and turning frequently. Add 12 small peeled **White On-ions** and 8 scraped and quartered **Carrots** for last 45 minutes of cooking. When done, thicken juices slightly with small balls of **Butter** and flour, blended together. Serves 4.

Tiny young turnips and mushrooms, served together with plenty of parsley and butter, are elegant with this too-often-forgotten dish. Pickles seem to be in order. And for dessert, try meringue shells filled with choco-late ice cream and topped with whipped cream.

pork

---

catch that aroma!
PORK STEAK IN CASSEROLE

Have your butcher cut a fresh **Pork Steak** about 1 inch thick (about 2 pounds). Brush it well on both sides with **Soy Sauce** and brown it quickly in 1 tablespoon **Bacon Drippings.**

Place it in a shallow casserole just slightly larger than the piece of meat. Cover it with a generous layer of thinly sliced **Onion.**

Combine 1 cup **Tomato Sauce** with ½ cup **Catsup,** 1 tablespoon **Soy Sauce,** 1 teaspoon **Sugar,** ¼ teaspoon **Pepper,** 1 tablespoon prepared **Horseradish** and a pinch of **Mace.** Pour this over the onions. Cover the casserole tightly and bake 1¼ hours at 350° F., until the meat is tender, basting several times with the pan juices. Serves 4 to 6.

With this savory dish, cornbread is superb. Let thinly sliced apples sautéed in butter and a cucumber salad round out the meal. And for dessert, serve pears with cheese or try pear dumplings.

THEODORE R. SILLS, INC.

Pork with sauerkraut and apples can be made with steaks or chops and either layered in a deep dish or spread in a shallow one.

---

sweet and sour

PORK STEAK WITH SAUERKRAUT AND APPLES

Have your butcher cut a 2- to 2½-pound steak from a fresh **Ham.** Brown it quickly in a little **Fat** in a heavy skillet.

Now arrange in layers, in a good-sized casserole, **Sauerkraut,** sliced **Apples,** peeled and cored, the pork steak, sliced **Onions,** more sauerkraut and a second layer of apples. Sprinkle each layer lightly with **Salt** and heavily with freshly ground **Black Pepper.** Dot the layers occasionally with **Butter** and dot the top one lavishly. Pour on **Sweet Cider** not quite to cover. Cover and bake 2 hours at 325° F. Serves 4 to 6.

Fix stuffed baked potatoes with a mixture of the potato, sour cream, cheese and a little mustard. Add salt and pepper to taste. Reheat quickly in the oven. Serve a green salad, perhaps with a green-onion dressing.

stag-night special
PORK CHOPS WITH SAUERKRAUT

Brown 6 **Pork Chops** quickly in a heavy skillet. Arrange a layer of **Sauerkraut** in the bottom of a **Buttered** casserole, then add 3 of the chops. Sprinkle with **Salt** some freshly ground **Black Pepper** and some bits of chopped **Garlic**. Repeat with more sauerkraut, the remaining chops and additional seasoning. Pour over all 1 pint of **Beer.** Cover and bake at 325° F. for 2 hours. Serve with mashed potatoes. For 4 to 6.

Have some raw celery and carrots with this, and some cucumber pickles. For dessert, serve baked apple dumplings.

sweet and spicy
PORK CHOPS WITH SWEET POTATOES

Prepare about 3 cups of whipped **Sweet Potatoes,** with plenty of **Butter** and a pinch of **Nutmeg** or **Mace.** Slice thinly 2 large **Onions;** pare, core and slice 3 tart **Apples.** Allow 1 large **Pork Chop** for each serving.

Now arrange in alternate layers in a buttered casserole the onions, sweet potatoes, pork chops and apples and top with sweet potatoes. Sprinkle each with **Salt** and **Pepper** and dot with butter. Dot the top layer with extra butter and bake 2 hours at 325° F. Serves 4 to 6.

Try a celery salad with mustard dressing and some good hot cornbread with this one.

educated ribs
BRAISED SHORT RIBS WITH MUSHROOMS

Arrange 6 pounds of **Short Ribs** in the bottom of a large, flat bowl or pan. Pour over them a marinade of **Soy Sauce,** 2 crushed cloves of **Garlic** and a generous grating of **Ginger Root** or, lacking that, a teaspoonful of

Ground Ginger. Let the ribs stand in this several hours or overnight. Then place them in a casserole and brown them for 15 minutes in an oven preheated to 500° F.

Now place under and around the ribs 1 pound of sliced fresh **Mushrooms** and 1 medium **Eggplant**, peeled and diced or sliced. Add ¼ cup **Sherry** and ½ cup of the marinade. Cover and roast 2 hours at 300°F. basting frequently and adding more marinade if needed. Serves 4 to 6.

Have some canned hominy cooked with butter and cream. Stewed tomatoes and onions would be good, too. Try fresh pears and apples with cheese for dessert.

worth the trouble
BRAISED SHORT RIBS WITH SESAME SEEDS

Have your butcher cut 6 pounds of **Short Ribs** into individual serving portions. Dredge these with **Seasoned Flour,** dip them in beaten **Egg** and then roll them in **Sesame Seeds** until they are thoroughly coated. Brown them quickly in **Butter** and then transfer to a casserole.

Add 1 cup **Tomato Purée**, 2 tablespoons **Chili Powder,** 4 cloves of **Garlic** (crushed or chopped fine), 2 tablespoons chopped **Parsley,** 1 teaspoon **Cumin Seed,** ½ teaspoon **Coriander** (fresh if possible) and 2 hot **Chili Peppers.** Add ½ cup **Broth,** cover and bake 2 hours at 300° F., basting frequently and adding a little more broth if needed.

Add ½ cup pitted **Ripe Olives** (whole or sliced) and ½ cup **Blanched Almonds.** Cook 15 minutes longer, or until the meat is tender. Serves 4 to 6.

If you're feeling adventurous, serve with polenta or tortillas. A cooling cole slaw wouldn't be amiss and, if you like beer, here's a good spot for it. For dessert, have cream cheese and guava jelly with crackers.

simply wonderful
HAWAIIAN HAM

In a casserole place a 1½-inch-thick **Ham Steak,** with edges slashed to prevent curling. Over the steak pour 1½ cups crushed **Pineapple.** Cover the casserole and bake at 325° F. for 1 hour and 15 minutes. Uncover, add 2 ounces of **Rum** and bake 15 minutes longer. Serves 4.

A sweet-potato casserole goes wonderfully well with this, as do some sautéed pineapple slices and garlic French bread. Have cheese, walnuts and crisp bread for dessert—and coffee in quantities.

something different
HAM LOAF

Combine 2 pounds ground **Smoked Ham** with 1 pound ground **Fat Pork.** Season with 2 teaspoons **Dry Mustard,** ¼ teaspoon **Cloves,** ½ cup **Mayonnaise,** ½ cup chopped **Parsley,** ½ teaspoon freshly ground **Black Pepper** and 2 beaten **Eggs.** Combine and top with **Pork Skin** or strips of **Salt Pork** and bake 1½ to 2 hours at 325° F., basting with **Pineapple Juice, Sherry** or **Vermouth.** Serves 4 to 6.

Excellent with this would be sautéed pineapple slices and fried sweet potatoes. Serve cheese and crisp bread for dessert.

light and tasty
HAM AND CHEESE PIE

Cream 3 tablespoons **Butter** until soft. Beat in 2 **Egg Yolks** until fluffy. Add ¾ cup grated **Parmesan Cheese,** 1 cup diced cooked **Ham** and 1 teaspoon **Mustard.** Then fold in 2 **Egg Whites,** beaten stiff. Pour all into a well-greased shallow casserole and bake at 350° F.

until puffy and lightly browned on top. Serves 2 as main course, or 4 as first course.

want a treat?
JAMBALAYA

Brown in a skillet 1 pound of lean cubed **Pork** and 1 large chopped **Onion** in 1 tablespoon **Butter** and 1 tablespoon **Olive Oil**. Just before the pork is done, add 1 pound cubed **Ham** and fry for 3 minutes. Place the meat and onion in a casserole. To the grease in the skillet, add 4 cups **Water**, ½ cup **Sherry**, 1 teaspoon **Dry Mustard**, ½ teaspoon **Celery Salt**, ½ teaspoon **Summer Savory**, ½ teaspoon **Thyme** and ¼ teaspoon **Black Pepper**. Cover the meat and onion with 1½ cups well-washed **Long-Grain Rice**. Bring the contents of the skillet to a boil and pour over the rice. Stir once into the ham and pork. Cover the casserole and bake at 325°F. for 40 minutes. Stir once with a long-tined fork about halfway through the cooking. Serves 6.

good and simple
SAUSAGES IN WHITE WINE

Combine in a casserole 1½ cups **White Wine**, 1 cup **Bouillon**, 1 cup diced **Carrots** and 16 small **White Onions**. Add **Salt** and **Pepper** to taste. Cover and cook 30 minutes at 350° F.

Meanwhile, brown some good-sized **Link Sausages** (the number depending on the size) in a skillet to render off part of their grease but not quite cook them through. Add them to the casserole when it has cooked half an hour; then cook uncovered for another 30 minutes, until the vegetables are tender and the sausages are cooked through. Serves 4.

Serve this with fluffy mashed potatoes with plenty of butter. Celery and endive stalks in place of salad, whole-wheat rolls and a lemon-meringue pie will fill out the meal.

good for everything
LIVER LOAF

Combine 1 pound each ground **Pork** and ground **Pork Liver.** Add 2 finely chopped cloves **Garlic,** ½ cup **Cognac,** 2 beaten **Eggs,** 1 cup soft **Bread Crumbs,** 1 teaspoon **Mustard,** 1 teaspoon **Salt,** 1 teaspoon freshly ground **Black Pepper,** and ½ cup chopped **Parsley.** Work all together well and form into a loaf. Place on a bed of **Bacon** or **Salt Pork Strips** and bake uncovered in an earthenware casserole 1½ to 2 hours at 325° F. Serves 6.

Eat hot with red cabbage, or cold, weighted down on top, with celery-root salad or potato salad. The loaf makes elegant sandwiches too.

lamb

---

fast favorite
LEFTOVER LAMB CASSEROLE

Sauté 2 medium **Onions,** cut in thin slices, in 3 tablespoons **Butter** until delicately browned. Combine with 1½ cups diced cold **Lamb,** 1 cup leftover **Lamb Gravy** or canned **Beef Gravy,** 1 clove **Garlic,** finely chopped, 2 cups cooked **Rice** and ¼ cup chopped **Parsley.** Correct the seasoning and bake, covered, at 350° F. for 45 minutes.

It's delicious served with buttered French peas and sliced ripe tomatoes with dill dressing. For dessert, try oven-baked apples with raisins and honey, and sour cream on the side.

fine and filling
BRAISED BREAST OF LAMB

Dredge in **Flour** and sear 3 pounds **Breast of Lamb**, cut in bite-sized pieces, in 4 tablespoons **Butter.** Remove to a casserole with 2 cloves **Garlic,** finely cut, 1 teaspoon **Salt,** 1 teaspoon **Black Pepper,** 1 cup **Tomato Purée,** ½ cup **Vermouth,** 2 thinly sliced **Onions,** a good pinch of **Thyme** and 4 **Carrots** cut in strips. Cover and bake at 350° F. for 45 minutes to 1 hour, or until the lamb is tender and the carrots cooked through.

Delicious with baked potatoes cooked in the oven at the same time, and watercress without dressing—this because the lamb dish is on the rich side.

Variation: Add 1 tablespoon **Chili Powder** and ½ cup ripe **Olives** to the casserole after ½ hour.

Louisiana choice
LAMB WITH OKRA

Cut 1½ pounds of **Lamb Shoulder** into serving-sized portions. Dredge with **Flour** and season to taste with **Pepper** and **Salt.** Brown quickly in ¼ cup **Olive Oil** and transfer to a casserole.

Add to the olive oil 2 finely chopped cloves of **Garlic** and 1 thinly sliced large **Onion.** Sauté for a few moments, then add to the meat. Add 1 pound of **Okra**— with the stems cut off—which has been soaked for half an hour in a quart of lightly salted **Water** with a little **Vinegar** added. Add 1½ cups **Tomato Juice** with the juice of 1 **Lemon.** Cover and bake at 350°F. for 1½ to 2 hours, until the meat is tender and well blended with the seasonings. Serves 4.

Serve this with browned rice cooked in the oven in another casserole.

while the season lasts
LAMB WITH ARTICHOKES

Chop 3 medium **Onions** and brown them lightly in 4 tablespoons **Butter**. Add to this 2 pounds of **Lamb Shoulder** or **Leg** cut into dice and lightly dusted with **Flour**. Brown quickly in the pan with the onions and transfer to a casserole. Add **Salt** and **Pepper** to taste, 1 or 2 finely minced cloves of **Garlic** and 1 tablespoon chopped **Mint**. Add enough **Water** or **Broth** to cover the meat and bake at 350° F. for 40 minutes, tightly covered.

Remove cover and add 3 **Artichokes** which have been carefully trimmed and cut into sixths, the choke sections removed, and carefully sprinkled with **Lemon Juice** so that they do not discolor. Cover the casserole with a piece of aluminum foil and place cover on top. Continue baking until the lamb is tender and the artichokes cooked—about 1 hour. Rectify the seasoning and serve. Serves 4.

This is excellent with either a rice pilaff or small new potatoes cooked in their jackets. For the salad, serve sliced tomatoes and paper-thin sweet onion slices with a vinegar and olive oil dressing, and this is a good spot for a dessert like lemon pudding.

a real delicacy
STUFFED SHOULDER OF LAMB

Prepare a **Bread Stuffing** for a boned **Shoulder of Lamb,** well seasoned with grated **Onion, Salt, Pepper** and **Thyme** and moistened (but not soggy) with melted **Butter** and a little **Vermouth.** Fill the shoulder and tie or skewer it firmly together.

Now arrange in the bottom of a large, deep casserole 12 small **New Potatoes,** well scraped, 12 small peeled **White Onions,** 6 little **Carrots,** scraped, 6 small peeled

Turnips, 2 cloves of **Garlic,** 1 pound of shelled **Peas** and 1 pound of Frenched **Green Beans.** Add a sprinkling of **Salt** and **Pepper** and a bouquet garni of thyme, **Parsley, Leek** and **Celery** tied together.

Place a grill in the pan so that it rests above the top of the vegetables. Put the shoulder of lamb on this and salt it lightly. If you have no grill that will fit the casserole, a trivet may be arranged to hold the lamb.

Add to the vegetables 4 tablespoons of **Butter** and 1½ cups of **Water.** Bring quickly to a boil on top of the stove. Cover and bake at 325° F., letting the lamb steam over the vegetables. Baste frequently with the pan juices and allow 20 minutes to the pound for your lamb. Let it rest 15 minutes before serving—with the lamb to be carved on a hot platter and the vegetables dished from the casserole. Serves 6.

This needs perhaps some greens—a salad or celery.

a change of pace
LAMB CASSEROLE MEDITERRANEAN

Cut 3 pounds of **Lamb Shoulder** into serving-sized pieces. Dust with **Flour** and brown quickly in ¼ pound of **Butter.** Add **Salt** and **Pepper** to taste. Arrange the pieces in a casserole and surround with a border of sliced **Tomatoes.** Add 2 finely minced cloves of **Garlic,** 1 teaspoon **Tarragon.** Weight the meat down with a heavy plate or lid. Cover and bake for 1 hour, at 325° F. Remove cover and plate and add 1½ cups **Rice** and enough boiling **Water** or **Broth** to cover the meat and rice (about 3 to 4 cups). Cover and continue baking until the rice is tender. Serves 6.
Variations

1. With Lettuce: Brown the meat and precook as above. Add 18 **Scallions** sautéed in the butter in which you sautéed the lamb, **Salt** and **Pepper** to taste, ½ cup **White Wine** and ½ teaspoon **Marjoram.** Cover and bake for 1 hour. Add 4 small heads of **Boston Lettuce,** which

have been cut in half and just wilted in boiling water for 3 minutes. Dot with **Butter.** Re-cover casserole and bake for 15 minutes.

Serve with **Rice** and a sauce made with 2 tablespoons **Lemon Juice** beaten over hot water with 2 **Eggs** and ½ cup of the juice from the casserole. But be sure to beat the sauce quickly so that it does not have a chance to curdle.

2. With Green Beans: Prepare lamb as above. Bake for 45 minutes at 375° F. Add 2 cloves of finely chopped **Garlic,** 1 pound of Frenched **Green Beans,** ½ teaspoon **Salt** and 1 teaspoon freshly ground **Black Pepper.** Cover tightly. Return to oven and continue baking for 35 to 40 minutes, until lamb is tender.

The only vegetable you will need with these casseroles is tiny French peas, in plenty of butter. Crusty bread would be good. If you like wine with dinner, a chilled rosé would give distinction to this meal. Dessert might well be sliced fresh or frozen peaches—perhaps with a touch of bourbon—and ice cream if you wish.

pâtés

---

perfect for summer
PORK PÂTÉ

Combine 2 pounds ground lean **Pork** with ½ pound ground **Salt Pork,** ½ pound **Pork Loin** cut in thin slices, 2 cloves minced **Garlic,** 6 finely chopped **Green Onions,** 1 teaspoon each **Salt** and freshly ground **Black Pepper,** ½ cup **Cognac,** and ¼ cup finely chopped **Parsley.** Let the meat stand for an hour with the seasonings. Then add ½ teaspoon **Thyme** and work it into the ground mixture.

Now line a casserole with slices of **Bacon** or **Salt Pork.** Add a layer of the ground meat, then a layer of the sliced loin. Sprinkle these well with additional cognac. Add the remaining ground meat and press down well. Top with additional strips of bacon or salt pork. Cover and bake 2 hours at 325°F.

Remove cover and weight the pâté down while it cools. Remove weights, re-cover and chill thoroughly before serving.

When sliced, this makes a very excellent first course, or it can be served for a luncheon or buffet.

perfect pâté
VEAL AND LAMB PÂTÉ #1

Combine 1½ pounds finely ground **Veal,** 1½ pounds ground **Pork,** 2 cloves finely chopped **Garlic,** ½ cup **Cognac,** 1 teaspoon each **Salt** and freshly ground **Black Pepper,** 1 teaspoon **Basil,** a pinch each **Rosemary** and **Nutmeg,** and 2 **Eggs.**

Line a large casserole with strips of **Salt Pork** or **Pork Skin**—available in pork markets. Add a layer of the veal mixture, then a layer of **Smoked Ham** or **Canadian Bacon,** sliced paper-thin, and a generous sprinkling of chopped **Green Onions** and **Parsley** mixed.

Repeat the layers until the casserole is filled, ending with the ground mixture at the top. Press down well and add an additional ½ cup cognac. Cover with more strips of salt pork and bake, covered, 2 to 2½ hours at 325°F. Remove the cover and weight the pâté down while it cools. Re-cover and chill before serving.

This may be kept for several weeks in the refrigerator if a layer of fat is kept on the upper and any other exposed surface in the casserole.

great stand-by
PÂTÉ MAISON

Combine 1 pound ground lean **Pork,** ½ pound ground fat **Pork Side Meat,** 1 pound chopped **Pork Liver,** 2 finely chopped cloves of **Garlic,** 6 finely chopped **Green Onions,** 1 teaspoon **Salt,** 1 teaspoon freshly ground **Black Pepper,** a pinch of **Nutmeg,** ½ teaspoon **Thyme** and 3 beaten **Eggs.** Blend all together thoroughly.

Line a round or oblong casserole with strips of **Bacon** or **Salt Pork.** Add the meat mixture, well packed down, and pour over all 1 cup **White Wine.** Press down again and top with additional strips of bacon or salt pork. Cover and bake 2 hours at 325° F., until thoroughly cooked through. It is best to set the casserole in another pan as it may boil over.

When done, remove from the oven. Uncover and weight the pâté down so that it will have a better texture. Cool and remove weight; then chill before serving. There will be a thin film of fat on and around the pâté. Do not remove this, since it keeps it better.

Slice for an hors d'oeuvre, cold luncheon dish or sandwiches.

a variation
VEAL AND HAM PÂTÉ #2

Grind 1½ pounds **Veal** with ½ pound **Pork.** Blend with 1 teaspoon **Salt,** ½ teaspoon each **Tarragon, Thyme** and **Paprika,** 2 cloves finely chopped **Garlic,** ½ cup chopped **Parsley,** 1 teaspoon freshly ground **Black Pepper** and ½ cup **Cognac.** Let this stand for 1 hour.

Grind 1½ pounds **Smoked Ham** and combine with 1 teaspoon **Dry Mustard,** ¼ teaspoon **Cloves,** ¼ teaspoon **Nutmeg,** and ¼ cup **Madeira.**

Knead the veal mixture well and divide into 2 equal parts. Line a casserole with strips of **Salt Pork** and add half the veal. Add the ham mixture and then the remaining veal. Press down firmly, top with additional strips of salt pork and pour on ½ cup more Madeira.

Cover the casserole and bake 2 to 2½ hours at 325° F. Remove the cover and weight the pâté down while it cools. Re-cover and chill.

Serve this elegant pâté with crisp buttered toast and a salad of celery root and mayonnaise. It makes a delicious first course or luncheon dish.

rabbit

---

from the fields
RABBIT NICOISE

Cut a **Rabbit** into serving portions and brown it well on all sides in **Butter.** Place it in a casserole with ½ clove of crushed **Garlic,** 2 tablespoons of **Olive Oil,** 1 pint of **Claret** and one jigger of **Cognac.** Sprinkle with **Salt** and **Pepper.** Cover and bake 1½ hours at 325° F.

Uncover and add 6 sweet **Italian Sausages,** which have been browned in butter, and ½ pound sliced **Mushrooms.** Cook ½ hour more and serve. Serves 4 to 6, depending on the meatiness of the rabbit.

Glazed white onions are good with this unusual dish, and to round out an unusual meal, you might try polenta. Red wine would go well, too.

venison

---

huntsman's reward
VENISON RAGOUT

Cut 3 pounds of **Venison** in pieces 1 to 1½ inches in size, removing gristle and any tough tissues. Soak in the following marinade: 2 cups of **Red Wine,** ¼ cup of **Red Wine Vinegar,** 2 cloves of minced **Garlic,** 2 chopped medium **Onions,** ½ cup of **Olive Oil,** 2 or 3 sprigs of

Celery Leaves, 3 ground **Juniper Berries,** ½ teaspoon of freshly ground **Black Pepper,** the juice and rind of a medium-sized **Lemon,** 1 small **Bay Leaf,** ⅛ teaspoon of **Thyme** and ⅛ teaspoon of **Oregano.**

Soak venison in this marinade for 24 to 48 hours in a cool place, turning occasionally to coat each piece well. Always remember that the marinade is a flavoring as well as a tenderizing device.

At cooking time, render ½ cup of **Salt Pork** cut in fine strips. Brown the pieces of venison in pork fat, then remove all together to a casserole with a tight cover. Add the marinade to the browned meat with 2 cups of **Tomatoes** (or 3 tablespoons of **Tomato Purée** with 1 or ½ cups of **Meat Stock**). Simmer 1 to 1½ hours or until tender. If the gravy needs moistening, add a mixture of half red wine and half stock as required.

When done, thicken with a paste of 1 tablespoon of **Butter** and 2 tablespoons of **Flour.** Taste for seasoning. Serves 6 to 8.

Serve this with wild rice with mushrooms and some buttered turnips. A hot mince pie gives you the perfect dessert.

3

POULTRY

Long, slow cooking in a tightly
covered casserole gives
you the essence of chicken,
duck or any other fowl

One of the earliest joys I can remember is eating chicken jelly, the perfect result of long, slow cooking. This method of preparing chicken, or any other fowl, brings out a rich, mellow taste, the very essence of the bird. Such exquisite flavor is found in many of the dishes presented here—dishes that take a minimum of work and a maximum of slow cooking in a tightly covered casserole. Not only the popular and versatile chicken, but turkey, duck, guinea hen, squab and other birds are included, offering a wide variety of choices for any occasion, whether it's a simple family meal or a large and elegant dinner party.

I suggest you try them first as they are presented, and then, using your own imagination, change the seasonings and flavorings to suit your fancy. You will be surprised at the many new twists you can give to the simplest recipes—this is the point at which cooking becomes an art.

best-dressed chicken
BAKED CHICKEN CASSEROLE

Singe, clean and cut up in serving portions a 4- to 5-pound **Roasting Chicken.** Dredge in **Seasoned Flour.** Melt 6 tablespoons of **Butter** in a skillet and brown the pieces of chicken on all sides, placing only a few pieces at a time in the pan.

Place the browned pieces of chicken in a casserole and reserve the fat in the skillet. Add to the casserole 12 small peeled **Onions,** 12 small scraped **Carrots,** 3 tablespoons of chopped **Parsley,** and a sprig or a pinch of **Thyme.** Cover with 2 cups of **Chicken Broth** made from the **Giblets.** Cover the casserole and bake at 350°F. for 45 minutes.

While the chicken is cooking, prepare the sauce. Add 4 tablespoons **Flour** to the fat in the skillet and blend well; you will need at least 4 tablespoons of fat, so add more if necessary. Add slowly 2 cups of **Milk,** stirring constantly, and cook over low heat until mixture thickens. Add **Salt** and **Pepper** to taste and a sprinkle of **Nutmeg.**

Serve baked potatoes, crisp and fluffy, to soak up the sauce. And a lightly tossed green salad is almost a necessity. Try some devil's-food layer cake to top it off.

use your leftovers
CHICKEN AU GRATIN

Place slices of cooked **Chicken** or **Turkey** in a casserole. Cover with butter-enriched **White Sauce.** Sprinkle with **Buttered Crumbs** and grated **Parmesan Cheese.** Brown in hot oven (400° F.) or under broiler.

Serve with fresh asparagus or broccoli, with lemon-

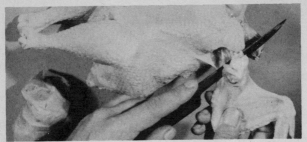

Cutting up a chicken: To remove the wings, pull each one out from the body and cut it away at the joint where it meets the breast.

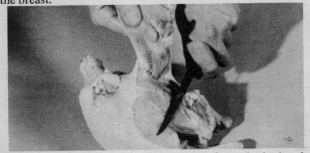

To remove the legs, pull each one away from the body of the chicken and bend it back until the joint of the thigh with the breast pops. Then free the thigh from the body. If desired, separate the thigh and drumstick.

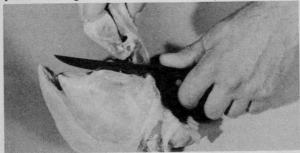

Grasp the back of the chicken and cut downward closely along the back to sever the rib connections.

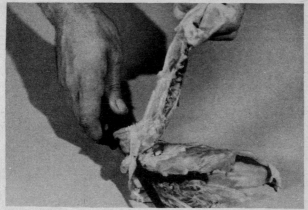

Then repeat the cut on the opposite side of the back, pulling the backbone free and cutting the connective skin and tissue at the neck. Discard the backbone.

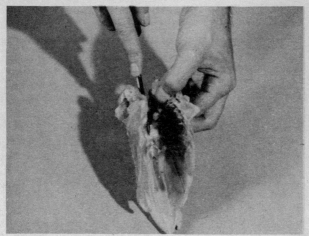

Nick the cartilage at the neck end as shown, cutting down through flesh and skin. Then pull the breast section apart and remove the large keel bone in the center.

butter. Shell macaroni with plenty of butter and grated cheese is fine for a change. Pears in red wine make an elegant dessert.

plenty of garnish
BROWNED CHICKEN CASSEROLE

Cut a 3- to 4-pound **Chicken** into serving portions and dredge well in **Seasoned Flour.** Brown quickly in 4 tablespoons **Butter** and transfer to a large casserole. Add 2 cups of **Chicken Broth,** cover and cook 15 minutes at 325° F.

Add 12 small **Carrots,** scraped, quartered and browned in butter, and 18 to 20 very small **White Onions.** Cover and continue cooking.

About 5 minutes before the chicken is cooked—it should take about 45 to 50 minutes all told—add 12 small **Mushroom Caps.** When the chicken is tender, add ½ cup of chopped **Parsley** and pour in slowly, stirring constantly, ¾ cup of **Heavy Cream.** Season to taste with **Salt** and **Pepper.** Serves 4.

Have a barley casserole with almonds, and some sliced ripe tomatoes. Angel cake with ice cream will make a fine dessert, and you will probably want good black coffee.

for grand affairs
CHICKEN GOULASH

Singe, clean and simmer until tender in boiling water a 6-pound **Chicken.** Add an **Onion** stuck with **Cloves,** 2 **Carrots** and a few **Celery Leaves** to the kettle. Season to taste with **Salt** and **Pepper.**

Cook 2 pounds of **Spaghetti** in the broth after the chicken has been removed. Cook until the spaghetti is tender—about 9 to 12 minutes.

Cut the meat from the bones and place in a casserole with the cooked spaghetti. Mix together 1 can of whole kernel **Corn** or 1 package of quick-frozen corn, 1 #2½ can **Tomatoes** or 1 quart home-canned tomatoes, 1 #2 can **Peas** or 1 package of quick-frozen peas, and 1 pound of sliced **Mushrooms.** Add to the chicken and spaghetti. Cover with grated **Cheddar** or **American Cheese** and bake in a preheated 350° F. oven for 45 minutes. Serves 15.

This is for a big buffet! Have a huge vegetable salad and with it a dressing bar—Russian, mayonnaise and French—all there and ready. Garlic bread is good as is a tray of assorted pickles. Pear upside-down cake made with a gingerbread mix is a fine dessert.

French art
COQ AU VIN

Singe, clean and cut a 4- to 5-pound **Roasting Chicken** in serving pieces. Melt 4 tablespoons of **Butter** in an earthenware casserole. Dredge the chicken pieces in **Seasoned Flour** and brown the pieces lightly in the casserole, using an asbestos pad over the flame.

Add 1 cup diced raw **Ham,** 10 small **White Onions,** peeled, 1 finely chopped clove of **Garlic,** ½ teaspoon of **Thyme,** a **Bay Leaf** and several sprigs of **Parsley.** Blend well so that all the ingredients are mingled. Pour a jigger of **Brandy** over all and blaze. Extinguish the flame with 2 cups of **Claret** poured over the chicken. Cover the casserole and cook at low heat until the chicken is very tender. Serves 4 to 6.

Start your dinner with thin slices of salami. Boiled potatoes and glazed onions are traditional with this casserole. And a good bottle of red burgundy is indicated with this French dish. For dessert, why not a light and creamy old-fashioned custard pie?

use your imagination

BRAISED CHICKEN IN CASSEROLE

Singe, clean and truss a 4-pound **Roasting Chicken.** Brown it very quickly in a large skillet, in which you have ½ cup melted **Butter** or ¼ cup **Olive Oil.** Turn the chicken on all sides so that it browns evenly. Add **Salt** and **Pepper** to taste.

Place the chicken in a large casserole and add the fat from the skillet. You may then add any seasonings you desire and a small amount of liquid—**Water, Broth** or **Wine**—and cover the casserole. Cook at 350° F. until the chicken is tender—about 1½ hours. Serve in the casserole with vegetables such as **Onions, Carrots** and small **Potatoes.** Serves 4 to 6.

Start your dinner with an avocado, stuffed with crab, and Russian dressing. Your vegetables, of course, are from the casserole.

all in one

CHICKEN CASSEROLE WITH RICE

Singe, clean and cut up a 3-pound roasting **Chicken** in serving portions. Rub pieces with **Lemon Juice,** then dredge them in **Seasoned Flour.**

Fry ¼ pound **Bacon** cut in slivers in a skillet till crisp. Remove the bacon to a casserole. Brown the chicken in the bacon fat, a few pieces at a time, so that it achieves an even color. Place in the casserole with 6 **Carrots,** scraped and quartered, 3 medium **Onions,** peeled and sliced, 1 large clove of **Garlic,** and 1 teaspoon of **Tarragon.**

Brown 1½ cups uncooked **Rice** in the skillet in which the chicken was browned, adding more fat if necessary. Add rice to the casserole with **Broth** made from the **Giblets** and **Neck** (2 cups or sufficient to cover completely) and ½ cup chopped **Parsley.** Place in a preheated 375° F. oven for 1 hour, until the rice is thoroughly cooked and the liquid is entirely cooked away. If the broth cooks away before the rice is soft, add a little more to the casserole. Serves 4 to 6.

This is a complete one-dish meal. Serve with it a bowl of radishes, green onions and celery. Hot rolls and sweet butter are always good.

in the pot
CHICKEN WITH LENTILS

Soak 2 cups of **Lentils** in 8 cups of **Water** overnight or 5 to 6 hours, unless you use the quick-cooking ones. Place the soaked lentils in a deep kettle with their soaking water—if not enough to cover about 1-inch, add boiling water. Add 1½ teaspoons **Salt,** 2 finely chopped cloves of **Garlic** and 1 **Bay Leaf.** Simmer gently until lentils are tender—about 1 hour, testing at 45 minutes.

Dredge one 4-pound **Roasting Chicken** cut up in serving portions in **Seasoned Flour.** Brown quickly in 6 tablespoons of **Butter,** salt and **Pepper** heavily, place pieces of browned chicken in casserole and cover with cooked lentils and liquid. If there is not enough liquid add a **Chicken Broth** or hot water in which you have dissolved 2 **Bouillon Cubes.** Cover casserole and bake at 350° F. for 1 to 1½ hours or until chicken is tender. Add additional liquid if the casserole cooks dry. Top with 5 slices of **Bacon** the last 15 minutes of cooking.

Small young heads of Boston lettuce, braised in butter, are excellent with this. And sour gherkins are an added touch. For an elegant but easy dessert, poach some peaches in a sugar syrup.

bird of paradise
STUFFED CHICKEN IN WHITE WINE

Clean, singe, stuff and truss a 4-pound **Roasting Chicken,** using this basic bread stuffing: Sauté 1 medium **Onion,** finely chopped, in 1 tablespoon of **Butter** till transparent. Blend with 3½ cups stale or toasted **Bread Crumbs,** 1 cup finely cut **Celery,** 1 teaspoon **Thyme** and **Marjoram,** mixed, 1 tablespoon chopped **Parsley.** Cut in ¼ cup butter or other fat. Add **Salt** and **Pepper** to taste.

Brown the chicken well in a skillet in **Olive Oil,** butter or **Bacon Fat.** Place in a casserole with ½ cup **White Wine.** Cover and place in a 325° F. preheated oven and cook for 45 minutes.

In the meantime, sauté 12 small **White Onions** and 15 small **New Potatoes** in the fat remaining in the pan in which you browned the chicken. Add salt and pepper to taste. The onions and potatoes should be nicely browned and partially cooked.

Remove the casserole from the oven and add the potatoes, onions, 12 **Mushrooms** and a good sprig of parsley. Salt and pepper the chicken, add another ½ cup of wine, cover and replace in the oven. Cook 1 to 1¼ hours until the chicken is tender. Serves 4 to 6.

Delicious with crisp slices of corn-meal mush sautéed in butter. Have tiny French peas with small white onions.

plenty rich
CHICKEN WITH NOODLES AND ALMONDS

Simmer until tender a 4- to 5-pound **Chicken** in lightly salted water to cover, with 1 sliced **Carrot,** 1 sliced **Onion,** 6 **Peppercorns** and half a **Bay Leaf.** Skin and remove the meat from the bones. Set the meat aside and return the skin and bones to the broth to cook for 20 minutes longer. Here, if you wish, add ½ cup **Dry White Wine.**

Boil ½ pound of **Noodles** until just tender—about 10 to 12 minutes. Drain, rinse with cold water and drain again.

Brown lightly ¾ cup **Blanched Almonds** in a little **Olive Oil.**

Now make a rich cream sauce using 4 tablespoons **Flour,** 4 tablespoons **Butter,** 1 cup strained **Chicken Stock** and 1 cup **Heavy Cream.** Add 1 tablespoon grated **Shallot.** Season to taste with **Salt** and **Pepper.**

Arrange the noodles, chicken and almonds in lightly packed layers in a buttered casserole. Pour on the sauce and bake 20 minutes at 350°F. Just before serving add several tablespoons of the chicken stock to moisten. Serves 4 to 6.

This casserole is on the rich side so accompany it with something simple—buttered string beans and crisp, hot toast. Baked custard could be your dessert, and coffee is always in order.

really complete meal
STUFFED CHICKEN IN CASSEROLE

Singe and clean a 4-pound **Roasting Chicken.**

Prepare a stuffing as follows: Cook 8 ounces of **Noodles** in 1 pint of **Chicken Broth** until tender. Add **Salt** and **Pepper** to taste. Drain and save the broth.

Sauté ¼ pound of chopped **Chicken Livers** and ¼ pound sliced **Mushrooms** in 2 tablespoons of **Fat** over a low flame for three minutes. Add to the noodles with ½ teaspoon **Nutmeg,** ½ cup grated **Parmesan Cheese** and ½ cup **Cream.** Blend well and stuff the chicken. Sew up the vent.

When the chicken is stuffed and trussed, brown quickly in 6 tablespoons of fat in a casserole. Turn the chicken on all sides to achieve an eyenness of color. Add 1 cup broth and cover the casserole. The broth used for cooking the noodles may be used if you desire. Place the casserole in a preheated 350° F. oven and cook for 1½ hours. Baste occasionally with a little broth —every 20 minutes should be sufficient. Serves 6 to 8, depending on the meatiness of the bird.

Broccoli with drawn butter is a fine accompaniment for this dish.

If you wish a thick sauce, rather than the pan gravy in the bottom of the casserole, melt 2 tablespoons of **Butter** in the juices of the chicken after it is done. Stir in 2 tablespoons sifted **Flour** blended with ½ cup **Milk.** Stir constantly over a medium flame till the sauce is thickened. Add salt and pepper to taste. Pour the sauce over the chicken in the casserole and continue cooking for 25 to 30 minutes, until the chicken is tender and the sauce has mixed well with the juices in the pan.

hawaiian touch
CHICKEN CASSEROLE WITH PINEAPPLE

Singe, clean and cut in quarters 2 2-pound **Broiling Chickens,** being careful not to splinter the bones. Melt 5 tablespoons of **Butter** or other fat in a skillet and brown the chicken well on all sides, adding **Salt** to taste. Place the chicken in a casserole with ½ cup of **Pineapple Juice** and place in a preheated 350°F. oven, covered, for 25 minutes.

Remove from the oven and add 1 cup of **Cubed Pineapple** and 2 thin slices of **Lemon.** Pour another ½ cup of pineapple juice over the chicken and re-cover. Replace in the oven for another 15 minutes. Test for tenderness. Add 1 cup of blanched, toasted **Almonds** and ½ cup pineapple juice. Remove the lid and cook for 5 minutes. Serves 4.

Baked sweet potatoes are fine with this. And serve grilled ripe tomatoes with fresh basil and a touch of olive oil. Instead of dessert, have some toasted French bread with cheese—some Brie or Schloss and perhaps some Liederkranz.

when company comes
CHICKEN CASSEROLE WITH SPAGHETTI

Singe and clean a 4-pound **Chicken.** Place in a kettle with some **Celery Leaves,** 3 **Carrots,** a sprig of **Parsley** and 2 teaspoons of **Salt.** Cover with boiling water and simmer until tender—about 1½ hours. When the chicken is tender, remove it from the broth and allow it to cool slightly. Remove all the meat from the bones and place it in a large casserole. Then proceed to the other ingredients:

Cook ¼ pound **Bacon,** cut in slivers, over a low flame until crisp. Remove the slivers of bacon and add to the chicken. Add 2 finely chopped medium **Onions,** 2 finely chopped cloves **Garlic** and ¼ teaspoon **Thyme.** Sauté until the onion is transparent but not brown. Add to the casserole.

While the onion is cooking, sauté ½ cup sliced **Ripe Olives** and 1 **Green Pepper,** cut into narrow strips, in **Olive Oil** in another pan. Salt to taste and add to casserole.

Melt 2 tablespoons of **Butter** in a skillet and add 6 large **Tomatoes,** peeled and quartered, and 1 teaspoon of **Sweet Basil.** Cook until well blended but not mushy. Add Salt and **Pepper** to taste and add to the casserole.

Cook 1 pound of **Spaghetti** in boiling salted water until tender—9 to 12 minutes. Remove this to the casserole and mix all the ingredients together with the spaghetti.

Beat 3 **Eggs** till lemon colored. Add ⅔ cup grated **Parmesan Cheese** to make a thick paste. Spread carefully over the spaghetti mixture and place in a 400° F. oven until the eggs and cheese are set and browned. Serves 8 to 10.

All that is needed with this is a bowl of raw vegetables with herbed sour cream, some crisp French bread, good butter and a cheese-board. A bottle of red wine would not be amiss here.

tasty and nourishing
CHICKEN CREOLE

Singe and clean a 5- to 6-pound **Fowl.** Cut in serving portions. Dredge in **Flour** and brown quickly in 6 table-

perfect for leftovers

SALMI OF CHICKEN, TURKEY OR DUCK

Sauté 2 finely chopped **Shallots** in 2 tablespoons **Butter** until just transparent. Add ½ cup **Dry Vermouth,** ½ cup pitted **Ripe Olives,** sliced or whole, and a pinch each of **Thyme** and **Rosemary.** Blend in 2 cups diced leftover **Game** or **Fowl** and 1 cup leftover **Gravy** or 1 can of beef gravy. Season to taste with **Salt, Pepper** and a little **Lemon Juice.**

Pour into a casserole and add 1 package of **Frozen Peas.** Bake 35 to 40 minutes at 350° F. Serves 4.

Try this with tiny boiled potatoes with chopped green onions, parsley, lots of butter, and serve a tossed green salad. For dessert, have raspberry sherbet.

glamor added

CHICKEN HASH MORNAY

Combine 2½ cups cooked, diced **Chicken** with 1 cup chopped **Mushrooms,** sautéed in **Butter.** Blend in 2½ cups hot **Mornay Sauce** and pour mixture into a well-greased casserole. Sprinkle with buttered **Crumbs** and grated **Cheese** and slip under the broiler to brown. Serves 4.

This will be good with a purée of spinach and some sautéed mushrooms. Have some crispy toasted fresh bread.

SAUCE MORNAY

To 1 cup of basic **Cream Sauce** or butter-enriched **White Sauce** add 1 **Egg Yolk** and ½ cup of **Grated Gruyere** or **Cheddar Cheese** with just a touch of **Mustard.** Stir over hot—not boiling—water until the cheese is melted and the sauce well blended.

to grace your table

WHOLE CHICKEN IN CASSEROLE, ANJOU FASHION

For 4 persons you will need a **Roasting Chicken** of 3 to 4 pounds, nicely fatted and plump. Brown it well in a casserole in melted **Butter** and roast it uncovered for 25 minutes at 400° F. to give it a nice color. Then add 6 slices of **Bacon,** cut in small pieces, 16 small **White Onions** and 16 very small **White Potatoes.** Add **Salt** and **Pepper** to taste and ½ cup **White Wine.** Cover the casserole, return it to the oven at 350° F. and cook for 45 minutes or until the chicken is tender and the vegetables are cooked through. Serve from the casserole if you are a clever carver.

You may substitute dry vermouth for the white wine in the recipe if you wish to.

Start your dinner with a little soup—perhaps a Vi-

Paella combines chicken with clams, shrimp and seasoned rice.

chyssoise. With the casserole, have tiny French peas in plenty of butter and perhaps a green salad. For dessert, try a sponge cake with hot chocolate sauce—and whipped cream if you want something really rich!

mediterranean touch
CHICKEN IN WHITE WINE

Dredge the pieces of 2 good-sized **Frying Chickens** in **Seasoned Flour**. Brown them quickly in **Butter** in a skillet, then transfer them to a casserole. Then add ½ teaspoon **Garlic Vinegar** and ½ cup **White Wine**. Cover and bake at 300° F. for 30 minutes. Add ½ cup pitted **Ripe Olives**, 1 can of **Pimentos**, chopped, 1 cup sliced fresh **Mushrooms** and 12 small **White Onions**. Correct seasoning. Continue cooking till the chicken and onions are done—about 40 minutes.

Blend 1 tablespoon of **Flour** with 2 cups of **Cream** and pour over the chicken. Cook until the sauce thickens, but do not let it boil. Peek at 10 minutes and then at 5-minute intervals. Serves 4 to 6.

the more, the merrier
PAELLA

Singe, clean and cut up a 3-pound **Chicken** as for fricassee. Wash 24 live **Clams** to remove all sand and grit. Clean 24 **Shrimps** by splitting shell and removing black vein.

Melt 5 tablespoons of **Fat** in a casserole. Brown the chicken in the hot fat, turning frequently to brown on all sides. Add **Salt** and **Pepper** to taste, 1 **Onion,** finely chopped, 1 thin slice of **Ham** cut in slivers and 3 hot **Sausages** cut in thin slices. Cook these together for several minutes, being careful to mix them well.

Add the shrimp, the clams in their shells, 3 diced **Pimentos** and a pinch each of **Saffron, Tarragon, Salt, Cayenne** and **Paprika.** Add 2 cups of raw **Rice** and cover the whole with 3 cups or more of hot **Broth** or boiling **Water** mixed with **Bouillon Cubes.** Place in a preheated 375° F. oven and bake until the rice is cooked and fluffy. If the liquid cooks away too quickly, add more hot broth, seasoned to taste. Top with freshly cooked **Peas**—1 package quick-frozen or 2 pounds fresh. Serves 6 to 8.

This elastic dish may be stretched by the addition of lobster, crawfish, crabmeat, turkey or pigeons. It is perfect for a large buffet.

an expert touch
BONED CHICKEN IN CASSEROLE

Have your butcher remove and save the bones from a 4-pound **Roasting Chicken** without cutting it in half;

have him leave the wing and the leg bones in place. You will reshape the chicken after stuffing.

Now make a court bouillon of the chicken bones, a **Knuckle of Veal,** cracked, a bouquet garni of **Thyme, Bay Leaf** and **Leek,** and **Salt** and **Pepper.** Add **Water** enough to cover the bones well and let simmer 1½ hours.

For the stuffing, mince well and blend together ¼ pound lean **Pork,** ¼ pound **Veal,** ¼ pound **Smoked Ham,** ½ cup **Buttered Crumbs,** 4 **Chicken Livers** and 3 **Shallots.** Season with salt, pepper and thyme. Stuff the chicken and sew up the vent. Then mold the bird into shape and tie it securely in a **Pork Casing** or a cotton cloth. (The pork casing may be procured at the butcher's.)

Drain the court bouillon into a medium-sized casserole. Place the chicken in this and let it poach, uncovered, for 1 to 1½ hours at 300° F. In the last ½ hour of cooking, add scraped quartered **Carrots,** peeled small **White Onions** and **Mushroom Caps** to the bouillon.

When this has been done, untie the chicken and return it to the casserole. Serves 4.

Serve with a rice pilaff with sautéed chicken livers and, on the side, asparagus with a vinaigrette sauce.

this will keep
CHICKEN MEXICAN

Cut a 5-pound **Chicken** or **Capon** into serving portions as for fricassee. Dredge in **Seasoned Flour** and arrange in a large, earthenware casserole which has been well greased with **Olive Oil.** Cook, uncovered, in a preheated oven at 500° F. for 20 minutes.

Lower the heat to 325° F. and add 3 finely chopped medium **Onions,** 3 finely chopped cloves of **Garlic,** 6 ounces of **Claret** that has been heated, 1 teaspoon **Sesame Seeds,** ½ teaspoon **Caraway Seeds,** a pinch each of **Mace** and **Marjoram** and 2 cups boiling **Broth.** Season to taste with **Salt** and **Pepper.** Cover and bake 30 minutes.

, Now add 1 cup **Blanched Almonds,** 1 cup pitted **Green Olives** and 4 tablespoons **Sweet Chili Powder.** Re-cover and bake 30 minutes longer, basting the chicken occasionally.

To thicken the sauce to the desired consistency, add a little **Corn Meal** mixed with cold water. In doing so, be sure to stir constantly till the thickening takes place, for the meal has a tendency to go to the bottom of the pot or casserole and stick there. Bake 20 minutes or so or until chicken is tender. Put aside and reheat when needed, for this dish is much better made ahead of time. Serves 4 to 6.

For this you might have some tortillas, frijoles refritos (refried beans) and sautéed green peppers. For dessert, why not serve a delicious baked caramel custard?

turkey

---

post-holiday wonder
TURKEY-SWEET POTATO PIE

Combine in a well-buttered casserole 3 cups diced leftover **Turkey Meat** with an equal amount of **Stuffing,** well crumbled. Beat 2 **Eggs** with 1 cup of **Milk,** ½ teaspoon **Salt** and ¼ teaspoon **Pepper.** Pour over the turkey mixture.

Mash 2 cups of cooked **Sweet Potatoes** and whip them till light and fluffy with **Butter.** Add pepper and salt to taste and a pinch of **Mace** or **Nutmeg.** Spread over the turkey and dot with additional **Butter.** Bake at 375° F. for 35 to 45 minutes. Serves 4 to 6.

Start this dinner with a good clear soup. Serve braised Brussels sprouts and celery with the main

course. Mincemeat turnovers for dessert could give
your meal a party touch, and cheese would add an extra
fillip.

interesting combination
TURKEY-OLIVE CASSEROLE

Have a 5- to 6-pound **Turkey** cut into serving pieces.
Dredge the pieces in **Seasoned Flour.**

Melt ¼ pound of **Fat** in a large skillet and brown turkey pieces, a few at a time. Place the browned pieces of
turkey in a large casserole. Add ½ pound of **Bacon,** cut
in tiny slivers, and ½ cup of chopped **Shallots** or **Green
Onions.** Add 2 cups of canned **Tomatoes** and 1 cup of
sliced, seeded **Ripe Olives.** Cover casserole and cook at
325° F. for 1½ to 2 hours, until turkey is tender. Taste
for seasoning. Serves 8.

Serve with hot cornbread and succotash. Start dinner with raw vegetables and leave them on the table.
Dessert should be light.

really exotic
ROAST TURKEY SESAMINE

Many of the shops specializing in chicken parts now
offer turkey parts for sale as well. For this dish select
those portions of the bird you like best—breast, wings,
second joints or legs. And the quantity is up to you.

Dredge the **Turkey** well in flour, then dip it in beaten
Egg to which you have added a little water. Roll the
pieces in **Sesame Seeds** until they are thoroughly and
thickly coated.

Brown them quickly in **Butter** on all sides, but do not
let the butter burn. Then transfer them to a large casserole, pour some **Cognac** over them and blaze.

Roast uncovered at 325° F. for 1½ hours, basting
occasionally with a mixture of **White Wine** and butter.

Then add about ¾ cup **Heavy Cream** to the pan. Blend with the pan juices and baste the turkey well. Return to the oven and cook for 20 more minutes.

Crisp fried potatoes with plenty of parsley are very good indeed with this turkey. And have a salad of cucumber, onions and tomato.

filling fare

CASSEROLE OF LEFTOVER TURKEY WITH RICE

Chop 2 medium **Onions** and sauté them in **Butter** or other **Fat** till just tender. Add ½ pound of sliced fresh **Mushrooms** and sauté for 2 minutes. Combine in a casserole with 2 cups diced leftover **Turkey**, ½ cup diced **Ham**, 1 cup crumbled leftover **Stuffing**, 2 tablespoons chopped **Parsley**, a pinch of **Thyme** and a sprinkling of **Salt** and freshly ground **Black Pepper.**

In the skillet in which you sautéed the onions, brown 1 cup raw **Rice** with 1 additional tablespoon fat and 1 tablespoon **Curry Powder.** Add the browned rice to the casserole and pour on 2 cups hot **Broth.** Place in a preheated oven at 375° F. and cook until the rice is tender and the liquid is absorbed. If the liquid is absorbed before the rice is cooked, add more; but heat it before you put it into the casserole. Serves 4 to 6.

duck

---

old-country savor

DUCK CASSEROLE WITH SOUR CREAM

Have a 5- to 6-pound **Duck** cut in convenient serving portions. Dredge the pieces in **Seasoned Flour** and brown them quickly in **Fat**; then remove them to an earthenware casserole and sprinkle with **Salt** and **Pep-**

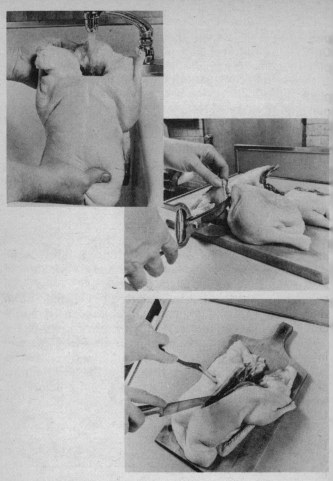

Three steps to quarter a duck: 1. Thaw duck thoroughly in its pouch, then remove bird from pouch. Take bag of innards from cavity. Rinse duck inside and out and pat dry with a towel. 2. Holding duck on a board with a two-pronged fork, use a heavy knife to cut along the side of the backbone from tail to neck to halve the duck. 3. With poultry shears sharpened to cut bone, cut halves midway between leg and wing joints.

NATIONAL DUCKLING COUNCIL

er. Add the giblets, chopped coarsely, 1 medium-sized
Onion, chopped fine, 3 tablespoons chopped **Parsley,** a
pinch each **Rosemary** and **Thyme** and a clove of **Garlic.**

Pour over all 1 cup of **Red Wine.** Cover the casserole,
place in a 350° F. oven and cook for 1½ hours. Add ½
pint **Sour Cream.** Blend with the pan juices and baste
the duck thoroughly. Re-cover and return to the oven
for 30 minutes, until meat is thoroughly tender. Serve
with fluffy rice. Serves 4.

western genius

DUCK CASSEROLE WITH PINTO BEANS

Soak 2 cups of **Brown Pinto Beans** in cold water
overnight. Drain and simmer them in lightly salted
water until just tender. Drain again and place them in a
casserole. Reserve liquid.

Have a 5 to 6-pound **Duck** cut into convenient serving portions. Dredge with **Seasoned Flour.**

Cut 3 strips of **Salt Pork** into small dice and fry in a
skillet till crisp. Place the bits of pork in the casserole
with the beans and brown the duck quickly in the pork
fat. Then transfer duck to casserole also.

Add thinly sliced medium **Onion,** a pinch of **Sweet
Basil,** a sprinkling of freshly ground **Black Pepper** and
½ teaspoon **Dry Mustard.** Next, put another layer of
beans into the casserole, and sprinkle on additional
seasoning. Add boiling water or bean liquid just to
cover and place in a 350° F. oven, covered. Cook until
the duck and beans are well done—1½ to 2 hours. Add
more water if necessary; but when done, the casserole
should not have too much liquid. Serves 4 to 6.

This would be excellent with some buttered turnips
and an endive and beet salad. And what better to wind
it up with than an apple charlotte?

most fragrant

DUCK CASSEROLE WITH CARAWAY AND RED CABBAGE

Have a 5- to 6-pound **Duck** cut into convenient serving portions. Dredge these well in **Seasoned Flour;** then brown them in 4 tablespoons **Fat** and transfer them to a deep casserole. Add 1 finely chopped **Onion,** a sprinkling of **Caraway Seeds** and a good pinch of **Sweet Basil.** Pour on ½ cup **Water.** Cover and place in a 350° F. oven for 30 minutes.

While duck is cooking, shred a medium head of **Red Cabbage,** discarding the hard center core. Add 2 tablespoons fat to the skillet in which the duck was browned and add the shredded cabbage. Let it cook down for 10 minutes, tossing it frequently with a fork. Add 3 tablespoons **Wine Vinegar,** 2 tablespoons **Brown Sugar** and **Salt** and **Pepper** to taste. Simmer 5 minutes more.

Combine the cabbage with the duck in the casserole. Cover and cook till the duck is tender—about 1 hour after the cabbage has been added. Serves 4.

Good fluffy rice should be fine with this casserole—with chopped green onions and raw mushrooms vinaigrette on the side. Crisp French rolls are always an addition. And for dessert, melon.

a really fine dish

DUCK IN RED WINE

Remove skin and fat from a 5- to 6-pound **Duck.** Cut duck into serving portions. Cook the skin and fat with the giblets and neck, simmering for about 1 hour. Skim off fat and reserve it.

In a large frying pan brown the pieces of duck over low heat in 2 tablespoons of duck fat. Place the browned pieces of duck in a casserole. To the fat in the frying pan add ½ clove of minced **Garlic** and cook for one minute. Stir in 2 tablespoons of **Flour.** Add 2 cups

NATIONAL DUCKLING COUNCIL

Quartering a duck before cooking makes it easier to serve.

of **Red Wine,** 8 sliced **Mushrooms,** 2 sprigs of **Parsley,** 1 small **Bay Leaf,** ½ teaspoon of **Thyme** and 1 teaspoon of **Salt.** Bring this to a boil, stirring constantly, until sauce thickens.

Place 8 peeled small **White Onions,** 8 scraped small **Carrots** and duck giblets in casserole with the duck. Top with sauce. Cover tightly. Bake at 350° F. until duck and vegetables are done—about 1¼ hours. Serves 4.

Barley, rice or wild rice would be a pleasant addition to this fine duck—and tiny new turnips in a generous amount of butter. An apple crisp or apple tart—hot and spicy—might be your dessert.

pheasant

---

tasty game bird
PHEASANT WITH SAUERKRAUT

Drain 2 pounds of **Sauerkraut** and place in a deep earthenware casserole. Add 2 cups of **Broth,** 1 cup of **White Wine,** a few **Juniper Berries** and ½ teaspoon of **Caraway Seeds.** Cover the casserole and simmer for 1 hour.

Singe and clean 2 **Pheasants.** Brown well on all sides in **Butter** or other fat. Add **Salt** and **Pepper** to taste. When the bird is thoroughly browned, place it in the casserole with the sauerkraut. Cover and place in a preheated oven at 350° F. and cook until pheasant is tender, about 35 to 45 minutes. Serve on a hot platter, surrounded with sauerkraut and fried hominy squares. Serves 4.

pigeon

---

native specialty
PIGEON CASSEROLE

Singe and clean 4 **Wood Pigeons.** Stuff with a small **Onion** and several sprigs of **Parsley.** Fry crisp 6 slices of **Bacon,** cut in cubes. Brown the pigeons in the fat very quickly with a clove of **Garlic,** cut very fine.

Place the birds in a deep casserole with 1 finely chopped medium onion, 1 sprig of **Thyme,** 1 pinch of **Basil,** 1 cup of sliced **Mushrooms** and 1 #2½ can of Italian-style **Tomatoes,** or 1 quart of home-canned tomatoes with 1 tablespoon of **Brown Sugar** added. Cover casserole, place in a preheated oven at 350° F. and simmer for 1½ hours. Taste for seasoning.

Buttered noodles are a must with this. Try some mashed yellow turnips, too. For dessert serve Indian pudding with ice cream.

4

FISH

If you watch your timing and
testing, these recipes
will give you fish dishes
fit for a gourmet

Nothing ruins good fish like overcooking. Cooked just to the moment when you can flake it easily with a fork or toothpick, it can be delicious. If done much beyond this point, it becomes mushy and flavorless—the dull food that causes so many people to say they do not care for fish. Therefore, as with soufflés, you must be careful with your timing and your testing.

Make use of the great variety of fish—fresh, frozen and canned—that you find in our markets. Try them in many different ways, with the addition of many flavorings and seasonings. Don't forget that any fish is better cooked with butter or good oil—use real butter, not substitutes, or either olive or nut oil. Fish takes well to herbs and certain customary flavorings such as garlic, onions and chives. Always treat fish with care when you prepare it, and you will have a tasty and elegant dish worthy of the finest restaurant. Everyone will come back for more.

try fresh salmon!
SALMON BAKED IN SOUR CREAM WITH DILL

Remove the skin from a 1½-pound **Salmon Fillet.** Sprinkle the fillet with **Salt** and a little freshly ground

NATIONAL MARINE FISHERIES SERVICE

Salmon fillets or steaks, baked in sour cream with dill, can be assembled ahead and baked when company comes.

Black Pepper. Lay it in a well-greased shallow casserole and surround it with **Potatoes** cut with a ball cutter and rubbed thoroughly with **Butter.**

Now combine 1½ cups **Sour Cream** (or more, if necessary, depending on the size of your casserole) with ⅓ teaspoon **Celery Salt,** 1 tablespoon grated **Onion** and 1 tablespoon chopped fresh **Dill.** Spread over the salmon and potatoes. Garnish with paper-thin slices of **Lemon** sprinkled with a little **Paprika.** Bake 30 to 35 minutes at 350°F. Serves 6.

A cucumber and onion salad is a must with this, as is crisp French bread and butter.

a meal in itself
SALMON CASSEROLE DINNER

Cut 1½ pounds of **Salmon Steaks** or **Fillets** into serving portions and sprinkle with **Salt** and a little freshly ground **Black Pepper.** In a well-greased large casserole, arrange in layers 1 cup **Whole-Kernel Corn,** 1½ cups cooked **Green Beans** and 2 cups sliced boiled **Potatoes;** sprinkle each layer lightly with more salt and pepper.

Combine ¼ cup melted **Butter** with 2 tablespoons **Lemon Juice,** 2 tablespoons grated **Onion** and 2 tablespoons chopped **Parsley.** Dip the salmon into this mixture and place on top of the potatoes. Now cover all with slices of peeled ripe **Tomatoes.** Pour on any remaining butter mixture and top generously with grated **Parmesan Cheese.** Bake 1 hour and 15 minutes at 350° F. Serves 6.

With this, nothing is needed but a salad; and there is no better salad with salmon than cucumber with a dill dressing. For dessert, lemon sherbet. And coffee!

out of a can
DEVILED SALMON

Drain and flake a 1-pound can of **Salmon,** removing all skin and bone and reserving the liquid.

Melt 2 tablespoons **Butter** and blend in 2 tablespoons **Flour.** Add the salmon liquid, with enough **Milk** added to make 1 cup. Cook gently, stirring constantly, until thick and smooth. Add 1 teaspoon **Worcestershire** and a dash of **Tabasco;** then stir in lightly 2 cups **Bread Cubes,** crusts removed, 1 tablespoon grated **Onion,** 2 tablespoons chopped **Green Pepper,** 2 chopped, hard-cooked **Eggs** and the flaked salmon. Place in well-greased individual casseroles.

Combine 2 tablespoons butter with ½ cup dry **Crumbs.** Sprinkle over each dish. Bake for about 20 minutes or until browned at 375° F. Serves 4.

Serve this with scalloped tomatoes baked in the oven at the same time. A salad of peas and tiny slivers of green onion with an olive-oil dressing is perfect. And for dessert—blueberries with ice cream and maple syrup.

easy to make
BAKED FLOUNDER IN CASSEROLE

Dredge **Flounder Fillets** (the number is up to you) well in **Flour** seasoned with **Salt, Pepper, Paprika** and **Thyme.** Brown them quickly on both sides in **Butter**— about 4 minutes. Then arrange them in a shallow casserole or baking dish and surround them with **New Potatoes** which have been boiled until just tender in their jackets, then drained and dried and rubbed with a mixture of butter and paprika. Bake 10 minutes at 400° F. and serve with a lemon butter-parsley sauce, which you make simply by adding lemon juice and parsley (with salt and pepper to taste) to melted or creamed butter.

This makes a fine simple luncheon or supper with an onion and green pepper salad, crisp buttered toast and a refrigerator cheese cake.

fit for a king!
FLOUNDER FILLETS WITH MUSHROOMS
AND ONIONS

Peel and parboil in salted water 12 small **White Onions.** Drain and set them aside. Clean and slice ½ pound small **Mushrooms** and cut 2 small **Carrots** in very fine, short strips.

Now arrange 4 good-sized **Flounder Fillets** in a buttered shallow casserole. Arrange around them the onions, mushrooms and carrots. Sprinkle lightly with **Salt** and a little more heavily with freshly ground **Black Pepper.** Add 2 tablespoons chopped **Parsley,** ¼ to ½ teaspoon **Rosemary** and 2 thin **Lemon** slices for each fillet. Pour over all ⅓ cup **Butter** melted with ⅓ cup **White Wine.** Bake for 20 minutes at 325° F., until the fish flakes easily with a fork.

With the fish, have plain boiled potatoes with parsley butter and a heaping platter of asparagus cooked just long enough so there's a bit of its crispness left. And the dessert suggestion is fruits and cheese.

try this for Sunday brunch
CODFISH AND SALT PORK

Soak 1 pound of **Salt Codfish** in cold water over-night. Drain and cut into small pieces. Fry out the fat from 1 slice, diced, of **Salt Pork.** Remove browned bits. Sauté 1 sliced **Onion** in **Fat** until just tender and add it to fish. In a greased casserole, arrange alternate layers of fish, 3 sliced medium-sized boiled **Potatoes,** 1½ cups cooked **Tomatoes** and 3 slices of salt pork, chopped. Top with **Buttered Crumbs** and a sprinkling of **Pepper.** Bake at 350° F. until brown. Serves 4.

for a perfect meal
FILLET OF SOLE

Blend 1 tablespoon **Butter** and 1 tablespoon **Water** in a skillet over low heat. Arrange 1½ pounds **Fillets** in skillet and sauté gently 8 to 10 minutes, turning them once. Remove the fillets to a hot shallow casserole. Add to the sauce in the hot skillet 1 more tablespoon butter, **Lemon Juice,** 1 tablespoon **Sherry** and 1 tablespoon **Heavy Cream.** Add **Salt** and **Pepper** to taste. Pour the hot mixture over the fillets and brown lightly under broiler. Serves 4.

for a delicate flavor
FINNAN HADDIE

Soak 2 pounds of **Finnan Haddie** in cold water for 1 hour. Drain. Then simmer fish for 30 minutes in fresh water. Drain again and separate into flakes.

Place in a shallow casserole and add 2 cups of

Cream Sauce, 1 tablespoon grated **Onion**, 2 table-spoons minced **Green Pepper** and 2 tablespoons chopped **Pimento**. Top with **Buttered Crumbs** and bake at 350° F. for 30 minutes, until browned. Serve with mashed potatoes. Serves 4.

a variation

FINNAN HADDIE DELMONICO

Cover 1 pound of boneless **Finnan Haddie** with boiling water and steam for 10 minutes over a low flame. Drain off the water and flake the fish.

Prepare a cream sauce by melting 4 tablespoons of **Butter**, blending in 4 tablespoons of **Flour** and gradually stirring in 1½ cups of **Light Cream**. Season to taste with freshly ground **Black Pepper, Paprika,** and **Salt** if the fish is not too salty. Continue stirring and cooking until the sauce is thickened and then combine with the flaked fish. Add ½ cup of **Grated Cheese** and pour into a buttered casserole. Top with **Buttered Bread Crumbs** and more grated cheese. Bake for 20 to 25 minutes in a 375° F. oven, or until the top is brown and crusty.

Serve with toasted protein bread, sliced cucumbers and onions with a vinegary dressing, and a dessert of baked pears with heavy cream. This finnan haddie dish is excellent for a Sunday brunch.

something different

BAKED FILLETS, POLISH STYLE

Oil a loaf tin well with **Olive Oil** or **Butter**. Sprinkle heavily with **Bread Crumbs**. Place in it, in alternate layers, 4 large **Fish Fillets**, 3 medium-sized **Onions**, sliced paper-thin and sprinkled with salt, 3 tablespoons chopped fresh **Dill** and a spreading of **Sour Cream**. Top with a layer of sour cream and mask the sides thickly with sour cream. Bake in a moderately hot oven

(375° F.) approximately 25 minutes, or until the sour cream is a golden color.

Unmold the loaf, sprinkle with chopped **Parsley** and chopped **Dill**. The onions will not be cooked through but will flavor the fish and be of an interesting texture. This should be portioned by cutting into slices rather than by lifting off the fillets. Serves 4.

This calls for boiled potatoes with plenty of butter, sliced tomatoes and cucumbers and toasted French bread. A hot coffee cake would be excellent for dessert.

old stand-by
BAKED FILLETS, PIONEER STYLE

Slice 2 medium-sized **Onions** very thin. Sauté in 4 tablespoons of **Butter** until just transparent. **Salt** to taste.

Oil a shallow casserole with 2 tablespoons **Olive Oil.** Arrange 4 **Fish Fillets** in casserole and season (see next page). Cover with sautéed onions and sprinkle with ½ cup buttered **Crumbs.** Bake in a hot oven (400° F.) 12 to 15 minutes, until fish is cooked. Sprinkle with chopped **Parsley** and crumbled crisp **Bacon.** Serve at once. Serves 4.

Serve this with tiny new potatoes or canned potatoes, and peas. A lemon-rice pudding would be good for dessert.

à la New Orleans
CREOLE HALIBUT

Sear a 2-pound **Halibut Steak** in a greased shallow casserole at 450° F. for 10 minutes. Reduce heat to 325° F.; dot halibut with 2 tablespoons **Butter** and sprinkle lightly with **Salt** and **Pepper.** Add ½ cup **Water** to casserole and cook for 20 minutes. Cover with creole

Creole halibut is a substantial fish dish with a Louisiana sauce of mushrooms, green pepper and tomatoes.

---

sauce (see following recipe) and cook 5 minutes longer. Serves 4.

CREOLE SAUCE

Sauté ½ cup minced **Onion,** ⅔ cup sliced **Mushrooms,** ¾ cup minced **Green Pepper** and 1 minced clove **Garlic** in 4 tablespoons **Butter,** until just tender. Add 2 cups canned **Tomatoes,** 1 cup condensed **Tomato Soup** and a bouquet garni of a **Bay Leaf, Parsley, Thyme** and **Cloves.** Blend in 1 teaspoon **Salt,** ¼ teaspoon **Pepper** and ¼ teaspoon **Paprika.** Simmer gently for 20 minutes. Remove bouquet and serve.

This calls for rice, which may be baked in the oven along with the fish. And why not continue the pepper flavor with sauteéd green peppers sprinkled with nutmeg? For dessert, a Nesselrode pie would be elegant.

dainty and delectable
HADDOCK WITH OYSTERS

Place 1 **Haddock Fillet** in a greased casserole and sprinkle with ½ teaspoon **Salt** and **Pepper.** Dip ½ pint **Oysters,** washed and cleaned, in 1 cup **Cracker Crumbs** and cover the fillet. Place 1 more haddock fillet on top of the oysters and fasten in place with toothpicks. Sprinkle with more crumbs and the juice of 1 **Lemon;** dot with 4 tablespoons **Butter.** Bake at 350° F. for ½ hour. Serves 4.

This delicacy might be preceded by some Vichyssoise. Have shoe-string potatoes with the fish and zucchini with garlic oil. For dessert, serve brownies and ice cream.

simply perfect
HADDOCK RABBIT

Place 2 pounds of **Haddock Fillets** in a greased casserole. Sprinkle with **Salt, Pepper** and minced **Parsley.** Make 1 cup of **White Sauce,** adding 1 cup grated **American Cheese.** Pour cheese mixture over the fish and bake at 350° F. for 35 minutes. Serves 6.

Start your meal with some ice-cold melon. With the fish, serve some boiled potatoes with parsley butter and artichokes with mayonnaise or French dressing. Chocolate layer cake (made from a mix) goes well for dessert. And coffee, of course.

hearty fish dish
FISH CASSEROLE WITH RICE

Heat 2½ cups of **Water** with ½ teaspoon **Salt** to the boiling point. Sprinkle in slowly ⅔ cup of **Cream of Rice** so that the boiling does not stop. Cook, stirring constantly, until smooth and slightly thickened. Lower the heat and let simmer gently for 5 minutes, stirring from time to time. Add ½ cup grated **Cheddar Cheese** and cook until the cheese is melted. Beat 1 **Egg** lightly and stir into it some of the hot cheese-rice mixture; then combine all and remove from heat. Let cool.

Melt 2 tablespoons **Fat** over moderate heat in a skillet, and sauté in it ¼ cup diced **Green Pepper** and ¼ cup diced **Onion**. Cook 5 minutes and add 1½ pounds **Haddock Fillets,** cut into cubes, 1 8-ounce can **Tomato Sauce,** 1 teaspoon **Soy Sauce,** 1 teaspoon **Sugar** and **Salt** and **Pepper** to taste. Let simmer 5 minutes, stirring from time to time.

Line the bottom and sides of a buttered shallow baking dish with the cooled rice mixture. Add the fish and vegetables. Bake at 375°F. until the fish is tender—about 35 minutes. Serve immediately. For 4.

This calls for a pleasant contrast—a cole slaw of red and white cabbage, hot biscuits or rolls and balls of raspberry mousse with cream for dessert.

Southern style
MARYLAND FISH CASSEROLE

Cut 1 pound of **Salt Pork** into fine dice and fry it in a skillet until crisp. Drain on absorbent paper and set aside, reserving the fat.

Now cut 3 pounds of **Fish Fillets**—flounder, haddock, rock cod—into 4-inch strips. Peel and slice 6 large **Potatoes** and 4 medium-sized **Onions.**

Pour the salt pork fat into a casserole and arrange alternate layers of fish, potatoes and onions. Sprinkle each with **Salt,** freshly ground **Black Pepper** and chopped **Parsley.** Pour over all 4 cups **Tomato Juice.** Cover and cook at 325°F. about 1 hour or until potatoes are tender.

Uncover before serving and carefully break 6 **Eggs** into the broth. Return to the oven till the whites are just set. Sprinkle with the crisp salt pork bits. Serves 6.

With this, try some sautéed cabbage, sweet and sour, and a cucumber and onion salad. For dessert, serve fresh or quick-frozen pineapple.

smooth and tasty
FISH PUDDING

Melt ½ cup of **Butter** in the top of a double boiler. Blend in ¾ cup **Flour;** add 1 pint **Milk** and **Salt** and **Pepper** to taste. Stir until smooth. Then beat in 3 well-beaten large **Eggs** and fold in 1 pound of boiled flaked **Cod.** Pour all this mixture into a well-greased casserole and bake at 350° F. for 45 minutes, until just firm. Serves 4.

New potatoes with plenty of butter and parsley and chives are a must with this. And serve a crisp cucumber salad and hot rolls. Have old-fashioned apple betty for dessert.

spicy!
DEVILED TUNA

In a mixing bowl combine 2 cups flaked **Tuna Fish,** 2 tablespoons chopped **Parsley,** 2 teaspoons **Lemon Juice,** 2 teaspoons **Prepared Mustard,** ½ teaspoon drained **Horseradish,** 2 chopped hard-boiled **Eggs** and **Salt** and **Pepper** to taste. Add 1½ cups rich **Cream Sauce.** Pour all into a well-greased casserole and top with **Buttered Crumbs.** Brown in a moderate oven (350° F.). Serves 4.

right off the shelf
TUNA-CHEESE CASSEROLE

Combine 1 13-ounce can of **Tuna Fish** with 2 table-spoons chopped **Stuffed Olives,** 1½ to 2 cups **Cheese**

Sauce and **Salt** and **Pepper** to taste. In a greased casserole arrange, in alternate layers, cooked and drained **Noodles** and the tuna mixture. Top with **Buttered Bread Crumbs** and bake at 350°F. for 20 to 25 minutes. Serves 6.

for Friday
OCEAN PERCH PIE

Thaw a 1-pound package of **Ocean Perch Fillets** and place them in 1 quart of boiling salted water. Reduce the heat and simmer for 10 minutes, until fish flakes easily with a fork. Drain and flake.

Now cook until tender 1 sliced large **Onion** in 2 tablespoons **Butter**. Blend in 2 tablespoons **Flour**, ¾ teaspoon **Salt**, ¼ teaspoon **Pepper**. When smooth add gradually 1½ cups **Milk** and cook gently until thickened, stirring constantly. Add 2 cups diced cooked **Potatoes**, ¾ cup grated **Swiss Cheese** and the fish. Stir a minute or two, then pour into a well-greased casserole.

Prepare a **Pastry Crust** and cover the casserole with it, sealing the edges and pricking the center in 2 or 3 places with a fork. Bake 20 to 25 minutes, until browned, at 450° F. Serves 6.

You might complement this with a crisp mélange of greens, raw mushrooms, croutons and a bacon-vinegar dressing. Try tiny pancakes with jelly for dessert or waffles with currant jelly and grated orange rind.

money-saving meal
GREEN PEPPERS STUFFED WITH OCEAN PERCH

Thaw 2 packages **Ocean Perch Fillets** and cut them into ½-inch pieces. Cut a slice from the top of 6 equal-sized **Green Peppers** and remove the seeds; parboil them in lightly salted water for 7 minutes, then drain. Fry 6 tablespoons diced **Bacon** until crisp; add 3 tablespoons chopped **Onion,** ¼ cup chopped **Celery,** ¼ cup **Chili Sauce,** 1 teaspoon **Salt,** ¼ teaspoon **Pepper** and the fish. Simmer for 10 minutes, then stuff into peppers.

Combine 4 tablespoons melted **Butter** (in which half a crushed **Garlic** clove has stood 10 minutes) with 1 cup dry **Bread Crumbs.** Spread half this mixture over the peppers. Remove a slice from the stem end of 6 ripe **Tomatoes.** Top the tomatoes with the remaining crumbs, pressing them in a little. Arrange peppers and tomatoes alternately in a shallow, well-greased casserole and bake 20 to 25 minutes at 350° F. Serves 6.

With a cucumber salad, French bread and sliced oranges and apples with grapes, this will give you a wonderful dinner.

shellfish

---

for royalty only
LOBSTER AU GRATIN

Sauté 2 cups of diced cooked or canned **Lobster Meat** in 2 tablespoons **Butter** for several minutes. Pour into a shallow casserole with a little **Salt** and a dash of **Tabasco Sauce.** Add 1 tablespoon each of **Sherry** and **Cognac** and ½ cup **Heavy Cream** blended with 2 to 3 tablespoons grated **Parmesan Cheese.** Sprinkle with **Buttered Crumbs** and more grated cheese and brown in a hot oven (375° F.) for 20 minutes. Serves 4.

With this serve noodles with butter and cheese, a cucumber salad and chocolate tarts.

gourmet's delight
ROCK LOBSTER DIVINE

Place 2 8-ounce South African **Rock Lobster Tails**— either thawed or frozen—into a kettle of boiling, lightly salted water. When the water comes back to a boil, lower the heat and cook, covered, for 1 minute longer than their weight. That is, cook an 8-ounce tail 9 minutes. Drain, then remove the meat. It can either be diced or left in chunks.

Cook 1 package of frozen **Asparagus Tips** until just barely tender. Prepare a cream sauce with 4 tablespoons **Flour,** 4 tablespoons **Butter** and 2 cups **Milk.** Season it with **Salt** and **Pepper** to taste, and blend in 1 tablespoon **Prepared Mustard** and 1 cup grated **Cheddar Cheese.** Stir until well blended.

Arrange the asparagus in a shallow casserole. Place the lobster meat on top and pour the sauce evenly over all. Bake at 450° F. until the sauce is bubbly. Serves 4.

This is excellent served with heated potato chips and some watercress. You might also have a crisp crusted apple pie with cream for dessert, along with plenty of coffee.

landlubber's lobster
ROCK LOBSTER CASSEROLE WITH MUSHROOMS

Cook 3 8-ounce South African **Rock Lobster Tails** in boiling, lightly salted water to cover. Dice the meat and save the liquor.

Melt 3 tablespoons **Butter** in the top of a double boiler and blend in 3 tablespoons **Flour,** ½ teaspoon **Salt** and ¼ teaspoon **Pepper.** Pour in slowly 2 cups of hot liquid—the lobster liquor, **Hot Milk** and the broth from 1 3-ounce can of broiled-in-butter **Mushrooms.** Stir until smooth and well thickened. Add 2 tablespoons **Tomato Puree,** the lobster and the mushrooms. When well blended, pour into a shallow casserole. Cook 5 inches below the broiler until the sauce is bubbly. Serves 4 to 6.

invite everybody!
DEVILED CRAB

Combine in a mixing bowl 1 pound **Crabmeat,** 1½ cups toasted **Bread Crumbs,** 6 thinly sliced **Mushroom**

Caps, 2 tablespoons of finely chopped **Onion,** 2 table-spoons of finely chopped **Parsley,** 2 tablespoons of finely chopped **Celery,** 3 **Eggs,** ½ cup of **Cream,** 1 teaspoon of **Salt,** ½ teaspoon of **Pepper,** and a few leaves of dried **Taragon.** Mix thoroughly and pile into individual ramekins, shells or a casserole. Top with bread crumbs and dot with **Butter.** Bake 15 minutes at 400° F. or brown under the broiler. Serves 4.

This dish and its neighbor, baked seafood in shells, make tasty first courses for company dinners and are just as good, if not better, for luncheon or Sunday night supper. When using them as the main part of your meal, serve them with hot potato chips and a salad.

a wonderful mixture
BAKED SEAFOOD IN SHELLS

Combine ½ cup small **Shrimp** (or large shrimp cut in small pieces) with ½ cup **Crabmeat** and ½ cup **Bay Scallops.** Sauté in 4 tablespoons **Butter** 4 to 5 minutes. Season with **Salt** and **Pepper** to taste. Combine with 1½ cups **Velouté Sauce** (thickened white sauce). Pile in a casserole. Top with additional sauce, sprinkle with buttered **Crumbs** and grated **Parmesan Cheese,** and brown quickly under the broiler. Serves 4.

Dixie delight
SHREVEPORT CRABMEAT

Melt 2 tablespoons **Butter** in top of double boiler; add 2 cups **Crabmeat** and **Salt** and **Pepper** to taste. Cook for 5 minutes over hot water. Mix ½ cup **Cream** with 2 well-beaten **Egg Yolks,** and add to the hot crab-meat. Cook 4 minutes over low heat, stirring constantly.

Pour into a casserole, sprinkling ½ cup grated **Cheese** over the top. Bake at 350° F. until cheese is

Baked seafood in shells can be made with a mixture of ocean treats, or with crab or scallops alone.

melted, and serve with **Lemon** wedges. Serves 4.

Serve this with French-fried or heated potato chips and a cauliflower cole slaw with slivers of green pepper.

for the discriminating palate
DEVILED OYSTERS

Shuck 36 **Oysters** and chop the meat.

Sauté 2 tablespoons minced **Onion** in 2 tablespoons **Butter** until tender. Blend in 2 tablespoons **Flour**. When smooth, add 1½ cups **Milk**, 1 teaspoon **Salt**, ¼ teaspoon **Nutmeg** and a few grains of **Cayenne**. Cook gently, stirring constantly, until thickened.

Add a few tablespoons of the sauce to 1 beaten **Egg.** Return egg mixture to the sauce, stirring well, and add the chopped oysters, 1 teaspoon **Prepared Mustard,** 1 tablespoon **Worcestershire Sauce,** 2 tablespoons chopped **Parsley.** Blend and fill the deep halves of the shells. Place in a baking dish and top each with well-buttered **Crumbs.** Bake 10 minutes, until browned, at 400° F. Serves 6.

to begin with
BAKED OYSTERS ON THE HALF SHELL

Shuck and drain 36 **Oysters;** place on the deep halves of the shells. Sprinkle with ½ teaspoon **Salt,** ⅛ teaspoon **Pepper** and 2 tablespoons minced **Onion.** Dot with 4 tablespoons **Butter.** Place the oysters in a baking pan and bake 10 minutes at 400° F., until the edges curl. Serves 6.

casserole classic
SCALLOPED OYSTERS

Arrange in a buttered casserole alternating layers of drained **Oysters** and crumbled **Soda Crackers,** beginning and ending with cracker crumbs. Sprinkle each layer of crumbs with bits of minced **Celery Leaves,** chopped **Parsley,** dots of **Butter,** a pinch or two of **Pepper** and a little **Salt.** (A little salt will go a long, long way.) When the casserole is full, pour in just enough hot **Milk** to keep the oysters moist. Bake at 400° F. for 30 minutes. Figure ⅔ cup or more of oysters for each serving.

an old favorite
OYSTER STEW

Sauté in **Butter** 1 pint of drained **Oysters** (canned or fresh) until their edges curl. Place oysters in a casse-

Oyster stew is one of the simplest first courses to prepare and its delicate flavor makes it one of the most elegant.

role and pour over them 1 quart of **Cream.** Add **Salt** and **Pepper,** a dash of **Worcestershire Sauce** and 1 large dab of butter. Bake at 350° F. until hot. Serve with an additional dab of butter in each cup if desired. Serves 4, but not as a main course.

5

MEATLESS DISHES

Once you serve these, you'll
never again think of
them as just substitutes for
meat—they're delicious!

It seems wrong to call delicious casseroles of eggs,
cheese or pasta "meat substitutes." They should not
be considered as a substitute for anything, for they are
quite capable of standing on their own merits. Eggs are
the perfect food and wonderfully adaptable to innumer-
able seasonings. Cheese—good, aged, natural cheese
—is the gourmet's delight, and has been a mainstay in
man's diet since ancient times. A well-browned cheese
casserole, hot and tangy, is magnificent eating. The
ever dependable pasta is age-old, too. No one knows its
origin, but according to most opinion, it came from
China. It is a most versatile food, and can be combined
with all manner of other foods and seasonings for
hearty and glamorous casserole dishes. It's popular all
over the world.

Try these recipes and see if you don't find yourself
selecting them from choice and not just as a substitute
for something else.

macaroni and noodles

old style, new twists
MACARONI AND CHEESE CASSEROLE

Boil ½ pound of **Macaroni** in 2½ quarts of lightly salted boiling water until just tender—about 9 minutes. Drain and transfer to a **Buttered** casserole. Pour over it 2 cups butter-enriched **White Sauce** and 1 cup grated **Cheddar** or sharp **American Cheese.**

Mix well and add **Salt** to taste. Sprinkle top with additional grated cheese and **Paprika.** Add **Buttered Crumbs** and bake at 375° F. for 20 minutes or until nicely browned. Serves 4.
Variations
1. Substitute 1½ cups **Heavy Cream** for the white sauce.

2. Substitute 1½ cups **Sour Cream** for sauce and add 1 tablespoon **Worcestershire Sauce.**

3. Use 1 cup diced **Ham** with the white sauce and the cheese. Add 2 tablespoons **Dry Mustard** to the sauce when you make it.

Use as a main dish or instead of other starch. Do not overcook.

goes with goulash
MACARONI CASSEROLE WITH SWISS CHEESE

Cook ½ pound of **Macaroni** in a quantity of rapidly boiling salted water until just tender—about 10 minutes. Drain, rinse and drain again. Arrange in alternate layers in a greased casserole with grated **Parmesan** and Switzerland **Swiss Cheese** and sprinklings of **Salt** and freshly ground **Black Pepper.** Top with an extra layer of cheese and **Buttered Crumbs.** Bake 20 to 25 minutes at 375° F. until the cheese is melted and the crumbs are brown. Serves 4.

This is good with any veal dish or with a beef goulash.

excellent light dish

MACARONI CASSEROLE WITH BASIL

Cook ½ pound of **Macaroni** in a quantity of rapidly boiling salted water until just tender—about 10 minutes. Drain, rinse and drain again. Place in a greased casserole with 2 tablespoons chopped **Parsley** and 1 tablespoon chopped **Basil.** Sprinkle over all ⅓ cup grated **Parmesan Cheese** and 2 tablespoons **Olive Oil.** Season to taste with **Salt** and **Pepper.** Toss all together and top with more grated cheese. Cover and bake 10 minutes at 375° F. Serves 4 to 6.

This is a good first course for a light dinner or an excellent accompaniment to pork or cold chicken.

for Friday lunch

MACARONI CASSEROLE WITH SALMON

Cook ½ pound of **Macaroni** in a quantity of rapidly boiling salted water till just tender—about 10 minutes. Prepare 2 cups cream sauce with 3 tablespoons **Butter,** 2 tablespoons **Flour** and 2 cups **Milk.** Season it to taste with **Salt** and **Pepper** and chopped **Fresh Dill.** Blend with **Canned Salmon** which has been well picked over for skin and bits of bone; and combine with the macaroni in a buttered casserole. Top with **Buttered Crumbs** and paper-thin slices of **Lemon** and bake 20 minutes at 375° F., until well browned. Serves 4 to 6.

Accompanied by cucumbers with dill mayonnaise and crisp French bread, this makes a fine luncheon or light dinner. Apples and pears and cheese for dessert!

ideal lunch

NOODLES WITH CHEESE AND SOUR CREAM

Boil ¼ pound of **Thin Noodles** in lightly salted water until just tender. Rinse in cold water and drain. Com-

Macaroni and cheese casserole—the universal budget stretcher, simple and scrumptious.

Noodles baked with cottage cheese and sour cream, with the tang of mustard and Worcestershire and a garnish of pimiento and olives, make a delicious party dish.

bine 1 cup **Cottage Cheese** with 1 cup **Sour Cream,** ¼ teaspoon **Pepper,** ½ teaspoon **Salt,** ¼ cup melted **Butter,** ½ teaspoon **Dry Mustard** and 1 tablespoon **Worcestershire Sauce.** Add to the cooked noodles and pour all into a well-greased casserole. Top with **Buttered Crumbs** and bake 1½ hours at 300° F. Serves 4.

This is a perfect dish for lunch. With chicken or veal scallopine, it makes a superb dinner.

delicious in itself
NOODLE CASSEROLE WITH SCALLIONS

Place ½ pound of **Noodles** in a quantity of rapidly boiling salted water and cook until just tender—10 to 12 minutes. Drain, rinse with cold water and drain again. Place in a well-greased casserole and set aside.

Melt 4 tablespoons of **Butter** in a skillet with 2 tablespoons of **Olive Oil.** Add 8 **Scallions** which have been chopped with about an inch of their green tops, and 1 tablespoon of **Tarragon.** Then sauté for 3 minutes.

Pour the melted butter and seasonings over the noodles. Toss all together until well mixed and season with **Salt** and **Pepper.** Top with grated **Parmesan Cheese** and brown in a hot oven before serving. Serves 4.

This is a delicious dish in itself. Start with some baked peppers and anchovies and serve a crisp salad, like endive, with several kinds of cheese. Have fresh fruit afterwards if you like.

fine Italian meal
STUFFED MACARONI IN CASSEROLE

The largest-size **Macaroni,** which is used for this dish, is available in most chain stores and in all Italian groceries. Boil ½ pound of this in lightly salted water for 8 to 10 minutes. Drain immediately and set aside to cool. It should be somewhat rubbery and not quite cooked through.

Have prepared a meat filling as follows: Grind 2 cups of any **Leftover Meat** with 1 clove **Garlic,** ½ teaspoon **Salt,** 1 medium **Onion,** ¼ teaspoon **Thyme** and 1 tablespoon **Parsley.** Blend with 1 beaten **Egg** and 2 tablespoons **Olive Oil.** Season with freshly ground **Pepper.**

Fill the macaroni with this mixture, using a fork or a teaspoon and leveling it at the ends.

Arrange these in a well-greased shallow casserole with 24 **Mushroom Caps** which have been lightly sautéed in oil or **Butter.** Pour over all 1 can—or more if necessary—of **Tomato Sauce** diluted with half its volume of **Broth, Consommé** or **Bouillon.** Sprinkle generously with chopped parsley and grated **Parmesan Cheese.** Bake 20 minutes at 350° F., until the sauce is bubbly and the cheese well browned. Serves 4.

With this pungent Italian fare I'd suggest an antipasto plate before dinner in lieu of salad, and some crisp French or Italian bread. Have a dressy dessert like a strawberry shortcake. And this is a good time for a bottle of red wine!

cheese and eggs

---

sunny side up
SCALLOPED EGGS WITH MUSHROOMS

Sauté ½ pound sliced fresh **Mushrooms** in 2 tablespoons **Butter** until just tender—about 4 minutes. Stir in 1 can condensed **Cream of Chicken Soup** and ¼ can **Water** or **Milk.** Add 2 teaspoons chopped **Parsley** and 2 tablespoons chopped **Celery.** Let simmer 5 minutes more.

Pour the sauce into a shallow casserole. Break in carefully 6 whole **Eggs,** spacing them as evenly as you can. Sprinkle with **Salt, Pepper** and a generous portion of grated **Parmesan Cheese.** Dribble over all some melted butter. Bake at 350° F. until the egg whites are set and the cheese lightly colored. Serves 6.

Serve with fried tomatoes and rice, or a tomato pilaff.

fine first course
CHEESE SAVORY

Make crusted bread cubes from 7 slices **Bread** and arrange alternate layers with ½ pound of **American Cheese,** cut in slivers, in a greased casserole. Beat 3 **Eggs.** Add ½ teaspoon **Paprika,** ½ teaspoon **Salt,** a pinch of **Dry Mustard,** 2 cups of **Milk** and ¼ cup **Sherry.** Beat all together and pour over bread and cheese. Bake at 325° F. for 1 hour. Serves 4.

This is a fine course for dinner—or for luncheon with a big salad.

for a light lunch
CHEESE PUDDING

Into a mixing-bowl pour ⅓ cup **Milk,** just barely heated, over 1 cup **Bread Crumbs.** Add 1 cup **Grated Cheese,** ½ teaspoon **Dry Mustard, Salt** and **Pepper** to taste and 2 well-beaten **Eggs.** Blend all together thoroughly and place in a **Buttered** casserole. Bake at 350° F. for 30 minutes. Serves 4.

Serve this for luncheon with a salad of greens and cherry tomatoes. For dessert, try something rich—an angel cake with some of the center torn into chunks, mixed with whipped cream and raspberries then forced back into the cake again. Top with raspberry-flavored whipped cream.

with cold meats
COTTAGE CHEESE PUDDING

Combine 1 pound of **Cottage Cheese** with 2 tablespoons chopped **Chives,** 1 beaten **Egg,** 2 tablespoons **Heavy Cream** and **Salt, Pepper** and **Cayenne** or **Tabasco** to taste. Place in a well-greased casserole and bake at 350° F. for 20 minutes. Serves 4.

This is a pleasant luncheon dish or a casserole to go with meats in summer.

fine first course
EGGS MORNAY

Cut 6 hard-boiled **Eggs** in half, lengthwise, and remove the yolks. Moisten the mashed yolks with a little **Mayonnaise** and add some **Minced Ham**. Season with **Mustard, Salt** and **Pepper**. Fill egg whites with mixture and arrange stuffed-side up in a shallow casserole.

Make a rich **White Sauce** and stir in ½ cup grated **Sharp Cheese**. Heat gently until cheese is well blended, then pour over eggs in casserole and brown in a hot oven or under broiler. More grated cheese may be sprinkled on top if desired, before browning.

Serve these delicious eggs as the first course for a big luncheon. Follow them handsomely with something like beef Bourguignonne, a salad, cheese and coffee. This dish would also be wonderful served with fresh asparagus for Sunday brunch.

something special
EGGS SHIRRED WITH MUSHROOM SAUCE

Sauté ½ pound sliced fresh **Mushrooms** in 2 tablespoons of **Butter** till just tender—about 4 minutes. Stir in 1 can of condensed **Cream of Chicken Soup** and ¼ can of **Milk**. Add 1 tablespoon of chopped **Parsley** and 2 tablespoons of chopped **Celery**. Simmer 5 minutes more.

Pour the sauce into a shallow casserole. Break in carefully 6 **Eggs,** spacing them as evenly as possible. Sprinkle with **Salt, Pepper** and a generous portion of grated **Parmesan Cheese**. Dribble some melted butter over all. Bake at 350° F. until the egg whites are set and the cheese lightly browned. Serves 6.

Try this for Sunday brunch. Serve with water cress, corn sticks, crisp bacon and coffee.

6

SOUFFLÉS

These are not only the most
glamorous casseroles,
they're also the most versatile.
And they're easy to make

The soufflé is the undisputed queen of casserole dishes. Light, puffy and brown, it is truly glamorous. But more important than its charm is its adaptability—it can be first course, main dish or dessert, depending on the flavoring used. A delicate clam soufflé makes an excellent introduction to an elaborate dinner. A sharp, tangy cheese soufflé is a delicious main dish for a luncheon or supper. A rich, creamy chocolate soufflé or a fluffy fruit soufflé makes the perfect finale for any meal.

For some reason, the average cook is terrified at the thought of making this dish. Such terror is mystifying, because a soufflé is actually easy to prepare. You must follow the rules carefully, of course, and give it your undivided attention, but that is true in preparing many other types of dishes. Here you will find basic soufflé recipes, easy to follow, to help you create these delectable casseroles with confidence.

king of the casserole
BASIC SOUFFLÉ MIXTURE

Melt 3 tablespoons of **Butter** in the upper part of a double boiler and blend in 3 tablespoons of **Flour.**

A fluffy cheese soufflé (this one made with Swiss cheese) is a true gourmet dish.

Gradually add, stirring constantly, ¾ cup of **Milk.** Stir until thickened. Remove from the fire and beat 4 **Egg** yolks into the mixture, blending thoroughly. Add ½ cup of **Sugar** and mix thoroughly. Flavor with 2 teaspoons of **Vanilla** and fold in the stiffly beaten **Whites** of the 4 **Eggs.** (Additional egg whites, if you want to be luxurious, will make the soufflé lighter.) Fold half the whites in first, rather thoroughly. Then add the rest, folding very gently. Be sure you fold; don't stir. Pour into a greased and lightly sugared casserole and bake in a 375° F. oven for 25 to 35 minutes, depending on the state of doneness you like. Some people prefer the French soufflé that is slightly runny in the center, and some want it well done all the way through.

Variations

1. Add ½ cup shredded **Ginger**——preserved or candied——to the batter before you fold in the egg whites. You can use the syrup from the ginger for sweetening instead of sugar.

2. Add 2 squares of unsweetened **Chocolate** melted over hot water and an additional ¼ cup of **Sugar.**

3. Add ¼ to ½ cup of any favorite **Liqueur.**

4. Add 2 teaspoons of grated **Orange Rind** and 4 tablespoons of undiluted **Frozen Orange Juice.** Or use **Lemon** instead of Orange.

5. Flavor soufflé mixture with your favorite **Spice,** or spices, to taste.

Serve any of the above with whipped cream or sweet dessert sauce.

The basic soufflé can also be the main course in a meal. Omit the sugar, add salt and pepper to taste and any of the following: chopped **Turkey** or **Chicken;** flaked **Fish;** flaked or chopped **Shellfish;** any left-over meats or fish. Anything added should be precooked, of course.

Other things may be added to give zest to the soufflé. For example, try adding a few chopped **Olives** with **Duck** or **Chicken.** Pieces of **Mushroom** or **Italian Roasted Peppers** are good in many meat or fish soufflés.

Serve any of the above main-course soufflés plain or with your favorite sauce: tomato sauce, cheese sauce, mushroom sauce or whatever you think would make a good combination of flavors.

good always
BASIC CHEESE SOUFFLÉ

Melt 3 tablespoons **Butter** in upper part of the double boiler. Add 2 tablespoons **Flour** and stir with a wooden spoon until well blended and smooth. Gradually add 1 cup scalded **Milk,** stirring constantly, and stir until mixture thickens and becomes smooth. Add 1 teaspoon **Salt,** a few grains of **Cayenne Pepper,** and ½ cup grated, sharp **Cheddar Cheese.** Continue stirring until cheese is melted.

Beat 4 **Egg Yolks** until light and lemon-colored, and pour the slightly cooled cheese mixture onto the egg yolks, stirring constantly. Cool for a short time.

While the cheese mixture is cooling, beat 4 **Egg Whites** very stiff; then fold into the mixture. Pour into buttered casserole and bake until well browned—35 to 40 minutes.

Be certain to have everyone ready, for this dish should be served at once. Serves 4.

perfect light meal
TOMATO SOUFFLÉ WITH CHEESE

Bring to the boiling point in a saucepan ½ cup **Tomato Juice** with ½ teaspoon **Salt.** Sprinkle in slowly 1 tablespoon **Cream of Rice** and cook over low heat 3 minutes, stirring constantly. Remove from fire and stir in 2 tablespoons **Butter** and ¼ cup grated **Cheddar Cheese.**

Beat 3 **Egg Yolks** till lemony and pour the tomato-cheese mixture over them, stirring constantly. Set aside and let cool.

Beat 3 **Egg Whites** until stiff but not dry and fold them into the other mixture. Pour all together into a lightly greased casserole or 1-quart baking dish and bake 35 to 45 minutes at 325° F. or until the soufflé is puffed high and golden brown. Serves 4.

Variation

Instead of the tomato juice, use ½ cup **Chicken Broth** (less salt if the broth is salted) and add ½ cup chopped

Mushrooms which have been sautéed until tender in butter. Proceed as above.

This is wonderful served with a celery, ripe olives and crisp, crumbled bacon salad and a mustardy dressing. For dessert, forget the calories and have a coconut cream pie.

good and healthy
SPINACH SOUFFLÉ

Blend 3 tablespoons melted **Butter** with 3 tablespoons of **Flour** in the top of a double boiler, stirring constantly. Add 1 cup **Milk** and continue stirring until the mixture thickens. Season with ½ teaspoon **Salt**. When mixture has cooled slightly, add beaten **Yolks** of 4 **Eggs** and blend well. Fold in 1 cup chopped cooked **Spinach**; and then gently fold in the beaten **Whites** of 5 **Eggs**. Place in a well-buttered 2-quart casserole and bake at 375° F. for 35 to 50 minutes until the soufflé is lightly browned and well puffed. Serve at once. Serves 4.

This dish is delicious served with sautéed mushrooms.

pretty special
BROCCOLI SOUFFLÉ

Melt 4 tablespoons **Butter** in the top of a double boiler. Add 4 tablespoons **Flour** and blend well. Add 1 cup **Rich Milk** and stir until thickened. Remove from heat and stir in 4 beaten **Egg Yolks.** Season to taste and add 1½ cups **Brocolli Purée**. Mix thoroughly over gentle heat and remove from fire again. Beat 4 **Egg Whites** until stiff and fold into the broccoli mixture. Pour into a buttered soufflé dish and bake at 375° F. for 35 minutes or until the soufflé has risen. Serve immediately. Serves 4.

This is a delicious luncheon dish. It is also something pretty special to serve with roast beef or roast lamb.

seafood delicacy
SALMON SOUFFLÉ

Flake well and remove skin and bones from 1½ cups cooked **Salmon.** Add ½ cup medium-thick **White Sauce,** 1 dash **Tabasco,** 2 teaspoons grated **Onion,** 3 beaten **Egg Yolks** and **Salt** and **Pepper** to taste. Beat 3 **Egg Whites** until stiff. Fold them lightly into the salmon mixture. Place in a greased casserole, which stands in a pan of hot water and bake at 350° F. for about 15 minutes. Serve with shrimp sauce, which you make by adding ½ cup of finely chopped cooked **Shrimp** to 1 cup of basic **Cream Sauce** or butter-enriched **White Sauce.** Serves 4.

from the sea
CODFISH SOUFFLÉ

Chop half a **Green Pepper** and half a medium-sized **Onion** and sauté in 2 tablespoons **Butter** until the onion is tender, not browned. Add 2 cups creamy mashed **Potatoes,** 1 cup cooked flaked **Cod** and 2 beaten **Egg Yolks.** Remove from flame and blend well. Then fold in 2 stiffly beaten **Egg Whites.** Place mixture in a greased casserole and bake in a 400° F. oven for 20 minutes. Serves 4.

For brunch, serve with crisp buttered toast and asparagus fingers, cream cheese and jam.

fine flavor
OYSTER SOUFFLÉ

Drain and chop 1 pint of **Oysters.** Melt 3 tablespoons **Butter** over gentle heat and blend in 3 tablespoons

Flour. Add 1 cup of **Milk** and cook, stirring constantly, until smooth and thickened. Remove from fire. When cooled a little, stir in 3 beaten **Egg Yolks** and the chopped oysters with **Salt** and **Pepper** to taste and a pinch of **Nutmeg.** Beat 3 **Egg Whites** until stiff but not dry, and fold into the oyster mixture. Pour into a buttered casserole and bake 30 minutes or until browned at 400° F. Serves 4.

Wonderful for a Sunday brunch. Or a perfect first course for dinner.

for a fine finish
LEMON SOUFFLÉ

Scald 1 cup of **Milk** in the top of a double boiler. Sprinkle in ¼ cup **Cream of Rice** with a pinch of **Salt** and let it cook gently 3 minutes, stirring constantly. Cover and let cook 5 minutes over very low heat. Stir in 2 tablespoons **Butter.** Set it aside to cool slightly.

Beat 3 **Egg Yolks** till thick and light. Stir in 1 tablespoon grated **Lemon Rind** and 3 tablespoons **Lemon Juice.** Add a few spoonfuls of the hot Cream of Rice mixture to the beaten egg yolks, blend, and then combine all together, stirring well and away from heat.

Beat 3 **Egg Whites** until stiff enough to hold a peak, then beat in slowly ⅓ cup of **Sugar.** Fold half at a time into the lemon mixture and pour into a 1½-quart casserole or baking dish which has had only the bottom greased. Bake 40 to 45 minutes at 350° F. or till puffed and golden brown. Serve immediately. Serves 4.

Variations

Orange Rind and **Juice** may be used instead of the lemon; or orange rind and 1 tablespoon orange juice and 2 tablespoons **Curacao;** or **Lemon Rind** and **Pineapple Juice.**

7

VEGETABLES

Casseroles and oven stews give
you vegetable dishes that
are delightful and different.
Slow cooking is the secret

Most garden vegetables are best when picked fresh,
cooked simply and quickly and served still a bit crisp.
Yet there are casserole dishes of vegetables, and oven
stews with vegetables, that are delightful in an entirely
different way. For example, a famous dish from the
south of France, called **ratatouille,** is a combination of
the best garden produce simmered for a long time in a
casserole. The fine flavors of onion, garlic, pepper, eggplant, tomato, squash mixed with oil, herbs and a touch
of vinegar are blended by slow cooking, sometimes for
days. Vegetables treated in this careful manner assume
the importance of a main course.

The variety of dishes in this section will give you a
wider enjoyment of vegetables and may lead you to giving them greater prominence in your menu planning. If
you have leftovers, try them cold, flavored with a good
oil-and-vinegar dressing.

if you're in a rush
HURRY-UP SUCCOTASH

In a casserole combine 1 can of **Kidney Beans** with 1 can of **Kernel Corn.** Add 6 tablespoons of **Butter,** ½ teaspoon of **Salt** and ½ teaspoon of **Chili Powder.** Cover and bake at 375° F. for 25 minutes or until well heated through and blended.

for company
CREAM SUCCOTASH

In a casserole combine 1 can of **Whole String Beans,** 1 can of **Small French Peas** and 1 can of **Kernel Corn.** Add 6 tablespoons of **Butter,** ½ cup of **Heavy Cream** and **Salt** and **Pepper** to taste. Cook at 350° F. for 30 minutes.

rich potpourri
PLAZA SUCCOTASH

Prepare 2 cups rich cream sauce with 3 tablespoons **Butter,** 4 tablespoons **Flour** and 2 cups **Milk.** When well blended, thickened and seasoned to taste with **Salt** and **Pepper,** add 1 cup each cooked **Lima Beans, Peas** and Frenched **String Beans.** Pour into a greased casserole and top generously with buttered **Crumbs** seasoned with a pinch or two of **Nutmeg.** Bake in a hot oven (400° F.) until crumbs are well browned. Serves 4 to 6.

This makes a fine accompaniment to veal or chicken.

goes with anything
SUCCOTASH CASSEROLE

Combine in a casserole equal quantities of freshly cooked **Lima Beans,** whole kernel **Corn,** and Frenched

Snap Beans. Cover with 1 cup **Sauce Mornay** (see next recipe)—or more if desired—and sprinkle liberally with **Buttered Crumbs** and grated **Parmesan Cheese.** Brown in the oven at 400° F. a few minutes before serving.

SAUCE MORNAY

To 1 cup of basic **Cream Sauce** or butter-enriched **White Sauce** add 1 **Egg Yolk** and ½ cup of grated **Gruyére** or **Cheddar Cheese** with just a touch of **Mustard.** Stir over hot—not boiling—water until the cheese is melted and the sauce well blended.

zestful side dish
STRING BEANS WITH SOUR CREAM

Pour 4 tablespoons **Olive Oil** into a casserole. Add 1½ pounds **String Beans** which have been cut, boiled in salted water until tender and drained; 1½ cups **Sour Cream; Salt** and **Pepper** to taste; and 1 tablespoon grated **Onion.** Combine this mixture well and sprinkle with dry **Bread Crumbs.** Bake at 300° F. for 30 minutes. Serves 4 to 6

a touch of elegance
STRING BEANS DUPONT

Place 2 pounds of Frenched **Green Beans** in boiling water, in which a piece of **Salt Pork** has been cooked 5 to 10 minutes. Cook beans until just barely tender, not limp. Drain beans, setting aside some of the cooking liquid. Place beans in a lightly greased casserole. Dice salt pork very fine and fry. Drain when crisp.

Melt 2 tablespoons **Butter** in the top of a double boiler. Blend in 2 tablespoons **Flour,** and add 1 cup **Milk** and ¼ cup of the vegetable liquid. Cook and stir until creamy. Then blend in ½ cup of grated **Sharp Cheese.**

Add **Salt** and **Pepper** to taste.

Pour this over the beans, sprinkle with more grated **Cheese** and with bits of the crisp salt pork and **Paprika.** Bake at 350° F. for 20 minutes.

This is delicious as a luncheon dish with cold meat. It could also be a full vegetable course or perhaps a first course at dinner.

vegetarian's delight
GREEN BEAN CASSEROLE WITH TOMATOES

Sauté 1 cup of chopped **Onion** in 2 tablespoons of **Bacon Drippings.** When light brown, add 2 cups of **Canned Tomatoes,** 1 cup of diced **Celery** and half a chopped **Green Pepper.** Season with 1 tablespoon **Sugar,** 1 teaspoon **Salt,** ½ teaspoon **Pepper,** 1 **Bay Leaf,** 1 tablespoon chopped **Parsley** and 1 crushed clove of **Garlic.** Simmer for 30 minutes, stirring frequently. Remove bay leaf and garlic.

Cook 1½ pounds Frenched **Green Beans** till tender. Place alternate layers of beans, tomato sauce and grated **Sharp Cheese** in a buttered casserole. Top with **Buttered Crumbs** and bake 25 minutes at 325° F. Serves 6.

Serve with hot rolls as a main course after a substantial soup. For dessert, try an angel cake heaped with sliced peaches (fresh or frozen) and whipped cream.

complements ham
CHEESE AND CORN

Combine together 2 cups cream-style **Corn,** ½ cup soft **Bread Crumbs,** ½ cup **Milk,** 2 beaten **Eggs, Salt** and **Pepper** to taste. Pour this mixture into a greased casserole and cover with 1½ cups grated **Cheese** and dry crumbs. Dot with **Butter** and bake at 350° F. for 35 minutes. Serves 4.

This is a fine partner for ham or chicken.

light and flavorful
CORN PUDDING

Melt 3 tablespoons **Butter** in a skillet and sauté 3 sliced **Onions** and 1 chopped **Green Pepper** till tender. Add 1 can cream-style **Corn,** ½ teaspoon **Salt,** ¼ teaspoon **Pepper** and a pinch of **Nutmeg.** Heat thoroughly and remove from fire. Stir in beaten **Egg Yolks.** Pour into a greased casserole and fold in 3 **Egg Whites,** beaten stiff. Bake 15 minutes at 300° F. until pudding sets; do not let it get too dry. Serves 4.

Serve with chicken or ham.

accompanies mixed grill
KIDNEY BEAN CASSEROLE

Cook a crushed clove of **Garlic** in 3 tablespoons of **Olive Oil** in a casserole. Mix in 1½ pounds **Kidney Beans,** boiled until nearly tender, ½ cup of **Red Wine,** 2 tablespoons of minced **Parsley,** and ½ cup of small, stuffed **Green Olives** cut in halves through their equators. Heat and serve with any grilled or broiled meat. Serves 6.

vegetarian's delight
KIDNEY BEAN CASSEROLE WITH ONIONS

Cook in a quantity of lightly salted water 1 pound of **Kidney Beans** with 4 strips of lean **Salt Pork,** 1 **Bay Leaf,** and 1 large **Onion,** grated. When beans are almost tender, drain them and discard the bay leaf.

Arrange them in alternate layers in a casserole with very thinly sliced **Onion.** Sprinkle each layer lightly with **Salt** and **Pepper** and generously with **Parsley.** End with a layer of beans at the top. Dice the salt pork and dot it over the casserole. Pour over all about ½ cup **Red Wine** for each cup of cooked beans. Cover and bake 30 to 40 minutes at 350°F., until the beans are tender. Serves 4 to 6.

These go well with chicken or duck. Or, with the addition of some crisp bacon, they are an excellent dish on their own. A great salad of tomatoes, onions and greens with an olive oil and vinegar dressing is a welcome side dish. And for dessert, serve a bowl of fresh fruits laced with grated coconut.

winter feast

KIDNEY BEANS AND SAUSAGE

Drain 4 cups canned **Kidney Beans,** reserving the liquid. Combine the liquid with 1 cup **Claret** and heat over a low flame. Blend together 2 tablespoons **Butter** and 2 tablespoons **Flour** and add to the liquid. Cook until mixture is thick and smooth, stirring constantly. Add 2 tablespoons minced **Parsley** and set sauce aside.

Form small cakes of ¾ pound **Country Sausage** and brown these in a separate skillet. Remove cakes and add to sauce. In the sausage drippings brown 1 large chopped **Onion** and ½ chopped **Green Pepper.** Add to the sauce 2 tablespoons drippings; season with **Salt** and **Pepper.**

Place the kidney beans in a casserole and cover with the sauce and sausage cakes. Bake at 350°F. for 30 minutes. Serves 6.

This casserole needs nothing more to accompany it than a cucumber, onion and tomato salad with a lemon vinaigrette sauce. Hot toasted bread might go along with it, too. And for dessert, pears baked in a ginger syrup and served with heavy cream.

leftover fowl

BROCCOLI IN CASSEROLE

Arrange slices of **Cold Chicken** or **Cold** or **Smoked Turkey** in a buttered casserole. Place cooked **Broccoli**

Stalks on the meat and cover generously with **Sauce Mornay** (see next recipe). Sprinkle with freshly grated **Parmesan Cheese** and **Buttered Crumbs**. Brown in the oven for 10 to 15 minutes at 350° F.

This is a delicious first course at dinner; it could be a separate course, for that matter, at almost any time. It is also excellent with cold meats for luncheon.

SAUCE MORNAY

To .1 cup of basic **Cream Sauce** or butter-enriched **White Sauce** add 1 **Egg Yolk** and ½ cup of grated **Gruyère** or **Cheddar Cheese** with just a touch of **Mustard**. Stir over hot—not boiling—water until the cheese is melted and the sauce well blended.

idea from abroad
SPLIT PEA WITH SAUTERNE

Combine 2 cups of puréed split **Green Peas** with 4 well beaten **Eggs**. Add to this mixture ½ cup **Sauterne**, 1½ teaspoons **Salt**, a pinch of **Cayenne**, 1 tablespoon grated **Onion** and 1 tablespoon chopped **Chives**. Blend thoroughly and pour into a greased casserole. Set the casserole in a pan of water and bake at 350° F. for 30 minutes. Serves 6.

tasty money-saver
PURÉE OF SPLIT PEAS

Soak overnight 1 cup dried **Split Peas** in 2 cups **Water**. Do not drain. Add 1 stalk diced **Celery**, 1 diced **Carrot**, ½ teaspoon **Salt** and ¼ teaspoon **Pepper**. Simmer to a thick mush and press through a sieve. Cut 3 **Bacon Strips** into small bits and fry until lightly browned. Remove from drippings and add to peas. Sauté 1 chopped **Onion** in drippings until tender and add all together to the peas. Blend thoroughly. Place in a greased casserole and bake at 350° F. 15 to 20 minutes. Serves 6.

adds to beef
SCALLOPED ONIONS

Butter a casserole thoroughly. Alternate, until casserole is full, a layer of sliced **Onions,** then a sprinkling of **Cracker Crumbs** dotted with butter and seasoned with **Salt** and **Pepper.** Add **Rich Milk** or **Cream** and dot with extra butter. Bake at 375° F. for 45 minutes.

This is good with beef or poultry.

to the king's taste
BAKED ONIONS

Peel medium-sized **Spanish Onions,** allowing 1 per person. Place in a buttered casserole with a very tight cover. **Salt** and **Pepper** well. Add ½ cup **Beef Bouillon** or **Consommé** and dot the top with **Butter.** Cover casserole and bake in a moderate oven at 350° F. for about 1 hour, until onions are just tender all the way through. Remove cover and sprinkle liberally with grated, sharp **American Cheese.** Return to oven uncovered or place under the broiler until the cheese melts.

swell for Sunday
STUFFED ONIONS

Parboil 4 large **Onions** for 20 minutes in boiling salted water. Drain and remove the center portion of the onions with a sharp knife and a fork. Fill the centers with well-seasoned **Sausage Meat** or **Link Sausages.** Place in a **Buttered** casserole and bake at 375° F. for 20 minutes until sausage is thoroughly cooked. Serves 4.

These are good with beef or turkey! Or try them for your Sunday brunch.

alongside steak!
SWEET AND SOUR ONIONS

Place 4 very large raw sliced **Onions** in a casserole. Combine 1 teaspoon **Salt** and ¼ cup each of **Cider Vinegar, Butter, Sugar** and boiling **Water**. Pour this mixture over the onions in the casserole and bake at 300° F. for 1 hour. Serves 4.

great with beef
ONION CUSTARD

Gently sauté in melted butter 3 bunches of **Scallions** cut into 1-inch pieces, until they are tender. Then let them cool. Line a medium-sized casserole with an unbaked **Pie Shell,** made from your favorite pastry recipe. Cover with the scallions.

Beat 3 **Eggs** lightly with 1 cup **Cream,** ½ teaspoon **Salt** and ⅛ teaspoon **Pepper**. Dice 3 strips of **Bacon.** Pour the egg mixture over the scallions and sprinkle with the bacon. Bake at 350° F. for 45 minutes. Serves 6.

goes with ham
BAKED ASPARAGUS WITH CHEESE

Grease well in **Olive Oil** a shallow oblong or oval casserole. Place 2 to 3 pounds freshly cooked, well-drained **Asparagus** in the dish. Sprinkle it with either ⅓ cup melted **Butter** or olive oil; then add a generous topping of grated **Parmesan** or **Swiss Cheese.** Coat with buttered **Bread Crumbs** and brown in a preheated oven at 400°F. until the cheese melts. Serve immediately. Serves 4 to 6.

This makes an excellent first course for a dinner. Or serve it as a luncheon dish with some fried ham and hot biscuits.

sour-creamed
BAKED MUSHROOMS

Remove the stems from 24 **Mushrooms** of as nearly equal size as possible. Clean the caps in acidulated water (1 teaspoon vinegar or lemon juice to 1½ quarts water) and place them in a **Buttered** glass casserole with a cover. Spread **Sour Cream** over the caps with a sprinkling of **Salt, Pepper** and **Lemon Juice.** Cover and bake 30 minutes at 300° F. Do not remove the cover till ready to serve. Serves 4.

easy to serve
STUFFED PEPPERS

When serving stuffed **Peppers,** allow 1 large or 2 small for each person. To prepare them, cut a slice off the stem end and remove all seeds and any thick grayish membranes. Rinse in cold water and parboil in lightly salted water about 5 minutes.

Any of the following stuffings may be used. They will serve 4 people, 1 pepper each. All are baked in a buttered casserole at 375° F. for 20 minutes.

Stuffings

1. Corn: Mix 2 cups fresh or cooked **Whole Kernel Corn** with ¼ cup melted **Butter** and **Salt** and **Pepper** to

taste. Fill pepper shells and top with buttered **Crumbs.**

2. Hash: To 2 cups **Corned Beef Hash**—canned or frozen—add 1 finely chopped medium **Onion,** 1 tablespoon chopped **Parsley** and 1 teaspoon **Dry Mustard.** Fill peppers and place in casserole.

3. Leftover Meat: Mix 1½ cups leftover **Chicken** or **Cold Meat** with ½ cup dry **Bread Crumbs,** 1 finely chopped medium **Onion,** ½ teaspoon chopped **Parsley** and 2 well-beaten **Eggs.** Fill peppers, cover with **Crumbs** and dot with **Butter.**

4. Curried Shrimp: Mix 1 cup cooked **Rice** with 1 cup cooked **Shrimp,** 1 tablespoon chopped **Onion, Salt** and **Pepper** to taste and 2 teaspoons **Curry Powder.** Moisten with **Heavy Cream.** Fill peppers and dot with **Butter.**

good buffet dish
SPINACH CASSEROLE WITH MUSHROOMS

Place 2 cups chopped, cooked **Spinach** in a greased 2-quart casserole. Add 2 tablespoons melted **Butter,** 1 teaspoon chopped or dried **Tarragon,** ½ teaspoon **Salt** and a few drops of **Lemon Juice.** Cover with 18 to 24 sautéed **Mushroom Caps,** depending on size. Over this pour very gently 4 well-beaten **Eggs** which have been mixed with ½ cup grated **Parmesan Cheese.** Bake at 350° F. until egg and cheese mixture is set. Serve at once. Serves 4.

This is excellent served with buttered noodles and ham.

try it with duck
CELERY CASSEROLE WITH ALMONDS

Remove the outer stalks and cut the leaves from 2 heads of **Celery.** Cut them into quarters lengthwise and brown the portions in **Butter** or **Olive Oil.** Place them in a shallow casserole with 2 **Green Peppers,** seeded and cut into slivers, a tablespoon each of chopped **Parsley** and **Chives,** ½ clove of **Garlic,** minced paper-thin, and 2 tablespoons olive oil. Top with ¼ cup shredded **Almonds** which have been lightly sautéed in butter and pour on 1 cup **Broth**—or enough for ¼ inch in the bottom of the casserole. Cover and bake 30 minutes at 350° F., basting several times. Uncover, baste again and cook till the celery is tender. Add a little more broth if necessary. Serves 4.

This dish goes splendidly with duck and pork.

outdoor idea
VEGETABLE CASSEROLE WITH HAM

Parboil 24 very small **White Onions** in lightly salted water till just tender. Drain and set them aside, reserving the liquor.

Drain and set aside 1 13-ounce can of **French Peas,** adding their liquor to the onion stock. (The size of these cans varies greatly but this is about the right amount.)

Now cut into very fine shreds enough **Virginia Ham** to make 1 cup. And shred 1 medium head of well-washed, drained **Boston Lettuce.**

Place the vegetables and the ham together in a casserole. Add 4 tablespoons of **Butter** and **Pepper** and **Salt** to taste to the combined liquors; cook down to about 1 cup. Pour into the casserole and toss the vegetables lightly so they are well basted. Cover the casserole and bake 20 minutes at 350° F. Uncover and toss again before serving. Serves 4 to 6.

This makes a splendid dish for outdoor eating, for it can be cooking in your kitchen oven while your main course is on the grill.

life of the party
STUFFED ARTICHOKES

Wash 4 large **Artichokes** and cut off about ½ inch from the tips of their leaves. Trim the stem ends level so that they will stand.

Now prepare the following stuffing. Combine ½ cup dry **Bread Crumbs** with ¼ cup grated **Parmesan Cheese**, ½ cup chopped **Parsley**, ¼ cup chopped **Chives**, 1 tablespoon grated **Onion**, ½ clove grated **Garlic** and 4 tablespoons melted **Butter**. Blend and press the mixture well down within the side leaves of the artichokes and into and across the top.

Stand them in an earthenware casserole with about ½ inch of water in the bottom. Dribble over them some **Olive Oil**. Cover and bake at 325°F. 1½ hours, or until they are thoroughly tender and the leaves pull away easily. Serves 4.

A wonderful first course for a party dinner. Or try them as a complete luncheon with a salad of greens and a ripe olive dressing.

with cold meats
ESCALLOPED EGGPLANT

Cook half a small chopped **Onion** and 1 shredded **Green Pepper** in 4 tablespoons of **Butter** until the onion is golden. Add 2 cups **Canned Tomatoes**, 1 teaspoon of **Salt** and a pinch of **Nutmeg**. Let simmer till well blended, stirring from time to time.

Peel an **Eggplant** and cut it into 1-inch cubes. Let the cubes soak 15 minutes in salted water, then press them dry. Add them to the tomato mixture and let simmer 30 minutes. Turn into a casserole, cover with buttered **Crumbs** and bake at 350° F. until the crumbs are brown. Serves 4.

Try this as a hot dish to accompany cold meats.

serve with eggs
EGGPLANT BAKED IN CREAM

Peel and slice 1 large **Eggplant** and brown the slices quickly in **Butter.** Place them in a shallow casserole, sprinkling each layer with **Salt, Pepper** and chopped **Walnuts.** Top generously with buttered **Crumbs** flavored lightly with **Mace.** Pour on **Heavy Cream** just barely to the level of the eggplant and bake 20 to 25 minutes at 325° F. Serves 4 to 6.

This is excellent as a luncheon dish with eggs or an omelet. You can vary it by adding pecan halves before baking.

Armenian touch
STUFFED EGGPLANT

Cut a large **Eggplant** in half lengthwise and parboil it for 10 minutes. Scoop out the pulp, leaving a good ½ inch of the shell. Chop the pulp very fine and add to it 3 tablespoons chopped **Chives,** 3 tablespoons chopped **Parsley,** 1 cup toasted **Bread Crumbs,** 1 cup diced cooked **Chicken** or **Turkey,** ½ cup **Pine Nuts** and seasonings to taste. Mix the ingredients together well and fill the shells. Sprinkle the top with some more of the toasted crumbs and dot very liberally with **Butter.** Bake at 375°F. for 20 minutes, until tender. Serves 4 to 6.

This makes a wonderful dish for supper. Or serve it for luncheon with a cream soup first, crisp toast, celery and radishes, and instead of dessert, some cheese.

Eastern delight
EGGPLANT MOUSSAKA

There are about a million ways of preparing this delicious casserole dish. We shall list only the basic recipe, and let you develop variations as you choose.

Moussaka is a Mediterranean classic combining eggplant and flavorful ground lamb. The dish is formed and baked in a mold.

Peel 2 large **Eggplants,** keeping the skin in large pieces. Cut their meat into cubes and sauté in 4 tablespoons **Olive Oil** and 3 finely chopped cloves of **Garlic.** Cover and simmer for 15 minutes. Add **Salt** and **Pepper** to taste.

Chop 2 cups of leftover **Lamb** (or any other meat) and combine with 1 **Onion,** finely chopped; 1 large or 2 small **Tomatoes,** peeled, seeded and chopped; 1 teaspoon **Thyme; Salt** and **Pepper** to taste. Blend this with the cooked eggplant, ½ cup of **Crumbs** and 2 slightly beaten **Eggs.**

Parboil the pieces of eggplant skin for 10 minutes. Line a casserole well with olive oil. Then lay in a layer of the eggplant skin so that the pieces overlap each other with the skin side out. (These should cover the sides as well as the bottom.)

Now add the eggplant-meat mixture together with ¼

cup **White Wine** or **Vermouth**. Dot with **Butter**. Cover and bake 35 to 45 minutes at 325° F. Remove from the oven and invert the casserole on a heated platter so that the Moussaka will turn out like a molded dish. Serves 4 to 6.

Have a casserole of rice, baked with chicken broth and a few pine nuts. For a fine dessert, serve an apricot Bavarian cream.

substantial lunch

EGGPLANT CASSEROLE AU GRATIN

Pare and slice 1 large **Eggplant** and 2 large **Spanish Onions.** Dredge the slices of eggplant in **Flour** and brown them quickly in **Olive Oil**. Add the onion slices and brown them.

Arrange in a casserole alternate layers of the eggplant and onion seasoned to taste. Sprinkle the top with chopped **Parsley** and cover with buttered **Crumbs**. Dot with extra **Butter** and bake at 350° F. for 25 minutes or until the vegetables are tender. Serve immediately. Serves 4 to 6.

This is a substantial luncheon dish with hot bread and some sort of substantial salad—kidney bean or shrimp, perhaps. For dessert, serve fresh fruit.

with lamb or mutton

EGGPLANT-TOMATO CASSEROLE

Pare and slice 1 large **Eggplant** and brown the pieces quickly in **Olive Oil**. Now arrange in alternate rows in a well-greased casserole the eggplant and 2 large sliced **Onions,** 3 large sliced peeled **Tomatoes** and 2 medium-sized shredded **Green Peppers**. Season each layer with **Salt** and **Pepper** and dot with **Butter**.

Pour ¼ cup olive oil over all when the casserole is filled. Place in a moderate oven (350° F.) and bake for 35 minutes, until tender. Sprinkle with grated **Parmesan Cheese** and return to the oven for 3 minutes. Serves 4 to 6.

Serve this with roast lamb, lamb chops or mutton steaks.

can't go wrong
STUFFED TOMATOES

Allow 1 large beefsteak **Tomato** for each person. Wash the tomatoes; do not peel, but remove the stem ends, pulp and seeds. Fill tomatoes with any of the stuffings listed below and place them in a **Buttered** casserole. Bake at 375° F. about 20 minutes.

1. Crabmeat (Cooked **Shrimp** or **Lobster** may be substituted): Combine 1 cup **Crabmeat** with ⅔ cup dry buttered **Bread Crumbs,** 2 well-beaten **Eggs,** 1 tablespoon chopped **Parsley,** 2 tablespoons chopped **Chives** or **Shallots,** ½ teaspoon **Salt** and a pinch of **Dry Mustard.** Fill the tomato shells, sprinkle with buttered crumbs and bake.

2. Rice: Sauté 1 cup chopped **Mushrooms** in 3 tablespoons **Butter** for 1 minute. Combine with ½ cup cooked buttered **Rice,** 1 tablespoon finely chopped **Onion,** 1 teaspoon **Worcestershire Sauce,** ½ teaspoon **Salt** and 1 tablespoon chopped **Parsley.** Fill tomato shells and sprinkle with buttered **Crumbs.**

3. Mexican: Sauté 2 medium-sized **Green Peppers,** finely chopped, in 3 tablespoons **Olive Oil.** Add ½ teaspoon **Salt** and ½ teaspoon freshly cooked or raw **Corn Kernels,** 1 tablespoon **Butter** and 1 tablespoon finely chopped **Onion.** Mix well. Fill tomato shells, sprinkle with buttered **Crumbs** and top with bits of **Bacon.**

All of these fillings will stuff 4 large tomatoes.

anchovy added

SAVORY STUFFED TOMATOES

Cut off the stem ends of 6 large **Beefsteak Tomatoes** and carefully remove the pulp, draining and chopping it. Brush the insides of the tomatoes with **Anchovy Butter.** Combine 4 well-chopped hard-boiled **Eggs** with 2 teaspoons chopped **Chives,** ½ teaspoon **Dry Mustard;** add chopped **Tomato Pulp.** Blend well. Fill tomatoes lightly with mixture, sprinkle with dry **Bread Crumbs** and dot with anchovy butter. Arrange tomatoes in a greased casserole and bake at 400° F. until browned. Serves 6.

Italian angle

PIZZA-STYLE CASSEROLE WITH VEGETABLES AND CHEESE

Combine 1½ cups **Milk,** 1 cup **Water** and 1 teaspoon **Salt** in the top of a double boiler and heat over hot water. Sprinkle in slowly ¾ cup **Cream of Rice;** cook, stirring constantly, until slightly thickened—about 1 minute. Cover and cook gently 10 minutes longer. Stir in 1 tablespoon chopped **Parsley** and a pinch of **Thyme.** Pour into a 9-inch layer cake pan, spread out thin, and chill until firm.

Meanwhile heat 3 tablespoons **Fat** in a skillet. Add ¼ cup chopped **Onion,** 1 minced clove **Garlic,** ¼ cup chopped **Celery,** ¼ cup chopped **Green Pepper** and ½ cup chopped or sliced **Mushrooms.** Sauté gently for 5 minutes. Add 1 11-ounce can condensed **Tomato Soup** and 1 cup grated **Cheddar Cheese.** Stir together until the cheese is melted.

Cut the chilled Cream of Rice mixture into 6 or 8 wedges. Arrange these on a greased 12-inch pizza pan or other flat baking dish. Pour the sauce over all and bake at 375° F. until lightly browned—about 20 to 25 minutes. Serve immediately with a salad. Serves 6.

This is very nice for luncheon. Serve some raw vegetables with it and a well-seasoned dunking sauce. A
platter of sliced salami and ham could be the meat.
Crown it all with coffee ice cream with a chocolate
sauce.

easy delicacy
SCALLOPED TOMATOES

Line a casserole with **Buttered Bread Crumbs.** Pour
over this one #2½ can of **Tomatoes** seasoned with **Salt,
Pepper** and a touch of **Basil.** Top with rolled **Soda
Crackers,** dot heavily with butter, cover and bake for 35
minutes at 350° F.

delightfully sharp
TOMATO CASSEROLE WITH CELERY
AND ONIONS

Cut enough stalks of **Celery** in paper-thin slices to
make 1 cup. Peel and slice thickly 4 good-sized **Tomatoes;** cut 3 **Onions** in slivers. Now arrange these in alternate layers in a buttered casserole, dotting each
generously with **Butter** and sprinkling with **Salt,** freshly
ground **Black Pepper** and a little **Basil.** Top with a layer
of **Crumbs** which have been browned in **Garlic** butter.
Bake at 350° F. for 35 to 45 minutes, until the vegetables are tender. Serves 4.

This is good with any dish that's fat or rich, for its
acidity cuts the richness.

most satisfying
CABBAGE CASSEROLE WITH SAUSAGE

Line a good-sized casserole with slices of **Bacon.**
Wash and quarter a **Cabbage** and place the wedges on

the bacon. Add 1 small **Onion**, ½ teaspoon **Salt**, ½ teaspoon **Black Pepper** and ½ cup **Bouillon.** Top with medium-sized **Pork Sausages** or **Italian Sausages.** Cover and place in a preheated oven at 350°F. Cook until cabbage is tender—about 1 hour. Serves 4.

This is hearty fare with mashed potatoes and sautéed apples.

glamorized favorite
BAKED CAULIFLOWER

Break 1 medium-sized head of **Cauliflower** into flowerets and cook them in lightly salted water until tender—about 15 minutes. Drain and arrange them in a buttered casserole. Dot with **Butter** and sprinkle liberally with grated **Parmesan Cheese;** add **Salt** and **Black Pepper;** top with buttered **Crumbs** and additional **Cheese.** Place in a moderate oven (375° F.) and brown for about 10 minutes.

Variations

1. Swiss: Cook and arrange the flowerets as above. Pour over them 1 cup of **Heavy Cream** and sprinkle them with coarsely ground **Black Pepper.** Add grated **Parmesan** and **Swiss Cheese** and top with buttered **Crumbs** and more cheese. Bake at 450° F. until they are nicely browned and the cheese is melted.

2. Cheesed: Cook a whole head of **Cauliflower** and drain and arrange in casserole as above. Dot it alternately with **Butter** and cubes of **American Cheese.** Bake in a hot oven (400° F.) until the cheese melts.

3. Bacon: Drain a 2 to 3 pound head of **Cauliflower** which has been cooked until just tender. Place it in a **Buttered** casserole and sprinkle it generously with buttered **Crumbs** and crumbled crisp **Bacon.** Sprinkle over all chopped **Chives,** chopped **Parsley** and **Salt** and **Pep-**

per. Bake 5 minutes at 425° F.
  4. Gruyere: See opposite page.

good with game
SAVOY CABBAGE AU GRATIN

Shred a medium-sized, well-washed head of **Savoy Cabbage** and remove all of the center core. Cook until barely tender—about 6 minutes—in boiling **Chicken Stock**. Then drain, reserving the liquor.

Now prepare a rich cream sauce with 3 tablespoons **Butter,** 2 tablespoons **Flour** and 1 cup each of **Milk** and the chicken broth. Blend with the cabbage in a well-greased casserole or baking dish. Top generously with buttered **Crumbs** and a few paper-thin slices of **Lemon.** Brown in a hot oven at 400° F. and serve immediately. Serves 4.

exquisite flavor
RED CABBAGE IN WINE

Wash thoroughly and remove the outer leaves from a medium-sized head of **Red Cabbage.** Cut and shred it as you would for cole slaw and place it in a casserole. Sprinkle it with **Salt** and a generous portion of freshly ground **Black Pepper.** Then pour on 1½ cups **Red Wine,** 1 tablespoon **Red Wine Vinegar** and 3 tablespoons **Soy Sauce.** Add 1 tablespoon **Sugar,** 1 crushed **Bay Leaf,** 2 tablespoons **Butter** cut in bits and, if you can buy it, a grating of **Fresh Ginger.** Toss all together and press down level in the casserole. Cover and bake 1½ to 2 hours at 300° F. Uncover and add, if necessary, just enough more red wine to moisten. Cook 20 minutes longer.

This is perfect with duck, goose or pork dishes.

---

try this outdoors
COTTAGE CHEESE POTATOES

In a well-greased casserole, place in alternate layers 2 cups diced cooked **Potatoes**, 1½ cups **Cottage Cheese**, 6 slices crumbled crisp **Bacon, Salt** and **Pepper**. Cover with **Buttered Crumbs** and brown under the broiler at low heat. Serves 4.

whipped delicacy
CHEESED POTATOES

Boil in salted water until tender 4 good-sized peeled **Potatoes**. Put them through a ricer into a mixing bowl with ½ teaspoon **Salt**, ¼ teaspoon **Pepper** and 3 tablespoons **Butter**. Whip all together and add **Heavy Cream** bit by bit till the potatoes are smooth. Fold in 1 cup grated **Sharp Cheese** and pile in a shallow casserole. Sprinkle the top lightly with additional grated cheese and brown in a hot oven (400° F.) before serving. Serves 4 to 6.

try this with chops
NEW POTATO CASSEROLE

Wash and clean some marble-sized **New Potatoes,** allowing 3 to 5 for each serving depending on their size. Peel or scrape a strip around each one about ⅜ inch wide. Place them in a casserole with melted **Butter**—allowing 1 tablespoon of butter for each serving. Cover tightly and bake at 375° F. for about 30 minutes, shaking the casserole from time to time to turn the potatoes and coat them with the butter. Test for tenderness and, if necessary, re-cover and cook till done. Serve with chopped **Parsley** or chopped **Chives,** or parsley and some crumbled crisp **Bacon.**

Lamb chops, veal cutlets or fried chicken take to this like natural allies.

fluffy delicacy
WHIPPED POTATOES EN CASSEROLE

Pile 3 cups of whipped **Potatoes** in a casserole. Then add ¼ teaspoon **Pepper** and ½ teaspoon **Salt** to ½ cup of **Whipping Cream.** Whip till stiff. Fold in ½ cup of grated **Parmesan Cheese.** Spread over the potatoes and bake at 350° F. until browned. Serves 4 to 6.

This casserole is marvelous with steak.

perfect accompaniment
POTATOES ANNA

Peel and slice thinly 4 large **Potatoes** or 6 medium ones. **Butter** a baking dish or casserole very thoroughly and place an even layer on the bottom. Sprinkle with **Salt** and **Pepper** and dot with butter. Add another layer of potatoes and repeat the process.

Now stand a layer vertically around the sides. Then add layers in the middle with salt and pepper as above until the potatoes are used up. Dot the top with an extra quantity of butter and bake in a hot oven (400° F.) 40 to 45 minutes, until the potatoes are thoroughly cooked and crusted a golden brown. These may be served either in the casserole or baking dish; or the dish may be inverted and the potatoes turned out on a platter. Serves 4.

This is a classic recipe. It is sure to become standard in your repertoire. It is the perfect accompaniment to a main dish of any meat or fish.

Scalloped potatoes become a full-meal casserole when baked with slices of sausage or cubes of cooked ham.

tasty and versatile
SCALLOPED POTATOES

Peel and slice thinly 1 medium-large **Potato** for each person to be served. **Butter** a baking dish well; arrange a layer of potatoes on the bottom, sprinkle with **Salt** and **Pepper** and dot with butter. Repeat this until all the potatoes are used. Then pour on **Milk** to just below the level of the potatoes and dot the top with an extra quantity of butter. Cover the casserole or baking dish and bake at 375° F. for about 30 minutes. Remove the cover and continue cooking until the potatoes are tender.

Variations

1. With Herbs: Sprinkle each layer with chopped **Parsley** and **Chives** mixed, and with salt and proceed as above.

2. Parmesan: Sprinkle each layer with grated **Parmesan Cheese** and dot with butter. Top with cheese and extra butter and proceed as above.

3. With Onion: Alternate layers with thinly sliced **Onion** and **Seasonings,** and proceed as above.

4. With Ham: Alternate the layers of potatoes with cubed **Ham,** sprinkle with chopped **Parsley** and salt and pepper and add 1 teaspoon of **Dry Mustard** to the milk before it is poured in.

5. Curried: Alternate layers of potatoes and **Onions.** Add 2 teaspoons of **Curry Powder** to the milk before pouring it in. Bake as above.

classic elegance
DELMONICO POTATOES

Dice 2 cups of **Potatoes** boiled until just tender. Make 2 cups of rich **Cream Sauce** seasoned with **Salt, Pepper** and **Celery Salt.** Arrange a layer of potatoes in a buttered casserole. Pour on half the sauce and sprinkle with ½ cup of grated **Parmesan Cheese.** Add another layer of potatoes, the rest of the sauce and more cheese (about ½ cup). Sprinkle with **Paprika** and dust generously with buttered **Crumbs.** Bake at 400° F. until sauce bubbles and crumbs are browned. Serves 4.

This classic goes with almost any meat.

fine for fowl
SWEET POTATOES

Boil 6 **Sweet Potatoes** until very tender. Mash and then whip with ¾ cup **Port,** 6 tablespoons melted **But-**

ter, 1 beaten **Egg** and **Salt** to taste. Pile in a casserole and brush with additional butter. Bake at 450°F. for 8 minutes. Serves 6 to 8.

a kick to it
SWEET POTATOES TIPSY

Place 2 cups hot, riced **Sweet Potatoes** in a mixing bowl with 3 tablespoons **Butter,** ½ teaspoon **Salt,** 4 tablespoons **Cream** and a few grains of **Pepper.** Beat all together till light and fluffy and then, bit by bit, pour in **Rum** or **Sherry** till the potatoes are almost creamy but still fluffy. Pile in a shallow casserole and brown in a hot oven before serving. Serves 4.

rice

---

want fluffier rice?
BOILED RICE

Wash ½ pound of **Carolina Rice** thoroughly. Cover it with cold water to about 2 inches above the rice. Add 1½ teaspoons **Salt.** Bring to a boil and boil for 15 minutes. Drain, toss it into a baking dish or an ovenproof serving dish which can be covered, and add 3 tablespoons of **Butter.** Cover and place in a moderate oven (350° F.) for 12 minutes. Do not stir. Lift lightly with a fork. Serves 6.

Variations

1 Steamed: Boil the rice for 14 minutes, then drain in a sieve and run cold water through it. Steam over boiling water for a few minutes before serving and toss with **Butter** and **Salt** to taste.

2. Creole: This is preferably made with the very **Long-Grain Patna.** Boil the rice for 14 minutes. Drain and toss into a **Buttered** pan or dish. Cover with **Parchment** or **Aluminum Foil** and keep hot for a few minutes at 300° F. This is ideal with curry dishes.

rice à la Near East
PILAFF

Like Creole rice, this is best made with the **Patna.** Wash the raw rice thoroughly, then drain and dry it in a towel. Chop 1 small **Onion** quite fine and brown it lightly in 4 tablespoons **Butter,** adding the rice just when the onion begins to brown. Toss the rice with a fork till it is just colored in the fat. Place in a baking dish or casserole. Add 2 cups of boiling **Bouillon** for each cup of rice, **Salt** and **Pepper** to taste, and a pinch of **Thyme** or **Oregano.** Cover and place in a 350° F. oven for 15 to 17 minutes, until the liquid is entirely absorbed and the rice just tender. Add melted butter before serving.

Variations

1. Saffron: Add a mere pinch of **Saffron** to the rice just when you turn it into the baking dish.
2. Moghul: Add **Toasted Almonds, Puffed Raisins** and **Peanuts** sautéed in oil and coarsely chopped, to a saffron pilaff. Top with additional toasted nuts and raisins and a circle of crisp **French-Fried Onions.** Serve with curry.

Italian delicacy
RISOTTO

The risotto is the Italian version of a pilaff. It is a main course with the addition of one or two other dishes; or it may be an accompaniment for certain meat dishes.

Carolina Rice is the best for this dish. Wash it thoroughly, then let it drain. Brown 1 medium-sized **Onion** lightly in 4 tablespoons of **Butter.** Add the rice and let it cook gently with the onion for 4 minutes, tossing it with a fork. Add 2 cups of boiling **Bouillon** for each cup of rice and **Salt** and **Pepper** to taste. Turn into a casserole or baking dish and bake, uncovered, 17 to 20 minutes at 350° F. Toss it very gently with a fork from time to time and when it is dry and tender, add melted butter and grated **Parmesan Cheese** to taste.

Variations

1. Milanese: Prepare as above. When you add the bouillon, add a pinch of **Saffron,** ½ cup small, raw **Mushrooms** and ¼ cup peeled, seeded and chopped **Tomato.**

2. Greek: Add small bits of **Garlic Sausage** or **Chorizo, Green Peas** and chopped **Pimento** or **Green Pepper** after the rice has been cooked.

3. Mediterranean: Add sautéed **Chicken Livers,** sautéed **Mushrooms** and slivers of **Ham** when the rice is removed from the oven.

4. Green Rice: Add 1 cup chopped **Parsley,** 1 cup freshly cooked, hot, buttered **Tiny Peas,** ¼ cup melted **Butter** and 1 tablespoon chopped **Chives** to cooked rice. Toss lightly.

fine with sea food
RICE PILAFF IN CLAM JUICE

Place 1 cup well-washed **Long-Grain Rice** in a casserole with 3 tablespoons **Butter,** 1 tablespoon chopped **Parsley,** 1 tablespoon chopped **Chives** and a dash of **Tabasco.** Add 3 cups **Clam Juice**—or half-and-half clam juice and **Chicken Broth**—and cover and bring to a boil quickly on top of the stove. Place in the oven at 300°F. and bake until all the liquid has evaporated—about 40 minutes. Serves 4.

Try this with boiled striped bass, a dry white wine, cucumbers in sour cream and dill, and tiny apple turnovers with sharp cheese.

barley

Barley is a much misunderstood and all-too-frequently neglected food. It is my contention that once you start to use it freely, you will forget all about wild rice, which is much more expensive. And barley may be combined with just about everything. Use it in quantities.

you'll adopt this idea
BASIC BARLEY CASSEROLE

Sauté ½ cup finely chopped **Onion** in 6 tablespoons **Butter** till just barely soft. Add ½ cup **Barley** and brown lightly with the onion. Season to taste with **Salt and Pepper** and pour into a casserole or baking dish. Add 1½ cups **Chicken Broth** or **Consommé**. Cover. Bake 30 minutes at 350° F. Add another 1½ cups broth and cook until the liquid is completely absorbed. Serves 6.

Variations

1. With Mushrooms: Add ½ pound sliced fresh **Mushrooms** which have been lightly sautéed in 4 tablespoons butter before adding the liquid.
2. With Chicken Livers: Add ½ pound **Chicken Livers** which have been quickly sautéed in butter.

3. Helen Brown's Chicken Gizzard Casserole: Cook until tender 1 pound of **Chicken Gizzards** in 8 cups water, with an **Onion** stuck with **Cloves,** 1 teaspoon **Salt,** a pinch of **Thyme,** a sprig of **Parsley** and a little **Celery** if available. This will take 1 to 2 hours over a moderate flame, depending on the gizzards. Add more water if necessary; you should have 3 cups left when finished cooking. When tender, drain the gizzards, reserving the broth. Slice them and sauté them with onions. Then proceed as in the basic recipe.

4. With Almonds: Proceed as in the basic recipe and add the sliced **Mushrooms** as in the first variation. After adding the liquid the second time, sprinkle the top of the casserole with ½ cup finely chopped **Toasted Almonds.**

5. With Pine Nuts and Herbs: Proceed as in the basic recipe. Add ½ cup finely chopped **Parsley,** ¼ cup finely chopped **Chives** or **Green Onion** and ½ cup **Pine Nuts.** Add **Hot Broth** and cook as directed.

6. For a turkey dinner: Prepare barley as in basic recipe. When it is ready to be served, top with ½ pound finely chopped sautéed **Mushrooms** which have been cooked in 6 tablespoons of butter and simmered down until almost black. Combine with ¼ cup chopped **Parsley** and ½ cup toasted **Almond** slivers. This is delicious with any game or poultry dish.

8

SOUPS

Oven cooking is tops for blending
flavors. With these
recipes you'll turn out the
most festive soups ever

Amazingly enough, few cooks realize the value of using the oven casserole in preparing soups. Yet most of them know that oven cooking is the perfect way to blend and mellow flavors—a most important point in soup-making. There is another reason why the oven does an excellent job in this field of cookery: it is far easier to maintain a low, even temperature in an oven than it is on the top of the stove.

Soups using legumes—such as dried beans or lentils—benefit especially from being cooked in this manner. They can simmer for hours with little or no attention, and the finished product is soft and rich in flavor. Many soups prepared in advance take on a festive quality if they are reheated in the oven at the last minute in little individual casseroles. This treatment makes even the most ordinary of soups seem delicious. Here are recipes for soups that are at their best when cooked in a casserole.

Chicken soup in the oven.

easy on the budget
LENTIL SOUP IN A CASSEROLE

Soak 2 cups **Lentils** overnight. In the morning place them in a deep casserole with 3 quarts **Water**, a **Ham Bone** or a **Lamb Shank** and 1 **Onion** stuck with **Cloves**. Add 1 tablespoon **Salt**, 1 **Bay Leaf** and 1 clove **Garlic**. Cover and bake at 350° F. for 2 hours. Reduce the heat to 250° F. and continue cooking for 2 more hours, until the lentils are practically a purée.

Remove and chop any bits of meat that remain on the bones. Just before serving add 4 **Frankfurters**, sliced thin, the chopped meat, ½ cup each chopped **Green Onion** and **Parsley**. Serves 8 or more.

Serve with or without a large dollop of sour cream.

soup-lover's dish
CHICKEN SOUP IN THE OVEN

At any grocery or butcher shop that sells poultry in parts, buy 3 pounds **Chicken Backs** and **Necks**.

Place the backs and necks in a large casserole with 1 **Onion** stuck with 2 **Cloves**, 1 tablespoon **Salt**, 1 teaspoon **Tarragon**, 1 teaspoon freshly ground **Black Pepper** and a sprig each of **Parsley** and **Celery**. Brown in a 400° F. oven for 30 minutes and then add 2 quarts **Water**. Cover and continue cooking for 3 hours at 300° F. Then take the casserole out of the oven.

Remove bits of meat from the bones. Strain the vegetables from the stock. Return the meat to the broth with ½ cup well-washed **Rice**, ½ pound chopped **Mushrooms**. Cover and continue cooking in the oven for 45 minutes. Serves 6 to 8.

Serve with chopped parsley and buttered toast.

hale and hearty

CABBAGE SOUP CASSEROLE

Combine in a casserole 4 strips of diced **Bacon**, 1 small head of **Cabbage** (about 1½ pounds) cut into eighths, 3 or 4 **Carrots**, scraped and quartered, 4 diced small **White Turnips**, 2 large sliced **Leeks** with a bit of their green tops, 1 tablespoon chopped **Chives**, 1 tablespoon chopped **Parsley**, and **Salt** and **Pepper** to taste. Cover with cold **Water** and cover casserole. Cook 3 hours at 270° F.

An hour before serving, add some **Potatoes** cut with a ball cutter, allowing about 6 little balls for each serving. When done, serve with sprinkling of grated **Cheese**. Serves 4.

Have loads of buttered toast with this.

meal in itself

CABBAGE SOUP IN THE OVEN

Place a large **Veal Knuckle** and 2 pounds **Shin** or **Brisket of Beef** in a casserole. Add 6 thinly sliced **Onions**, 3 thinly sliced **Carrots**, 1 clove **Garlic**, 1 tablespoon **Salt** and 1 teaspoon **Rosemary**. Brown quickly in a 450° F. oven. Add 2 quarts **Water**, cover, and continue baking at 300° F. for 2 hours.

Remove the casserole and add 1 medium head **Cabbage**, thinly shredded, 1 teaspoon **Salt**, and 1 can **Garbanzos** (chick peas). Cover casserole and continue cooking in the oven for 1 hour at 300° F. Remove and serve from the casserole. Serves 8.

9

DESSERTS

If you are looking for a
change from pie and
cake, here's a variety of light,
easy-to-prepare desserts

Dessert casseroles are growing in popularity. They are certainly a welcome change from the usual pie or cake; they appeal to the large number of people who prefer lighter foods in this era of leisurely living; many of them are quick and easy to prepare, making the cook's work simpler. An oven dessert can cook beside the meat or vegetable casserole, or if the dessert is quick-cooking and served hot, it can be popped into the oven as the first course is brought to the table. It will cook away while the rest of the dinner is being enjoyed.

Here you will find recipes for a variety of these dishes, some that can be prepared well in advance—even the day before—and others that can be whipped up quickly at the last minute. Included are many interesting ways to cook fruit in the oven. Just try some of these suggestions and see how delicious and flavorful fruit can be.

love that aroma!
OLD-FASHIONED BROWN BETTY

Butter a fairly deep casserole and place in it a layer of peeled, cored **Tart Apples** sliced quite thin. (Figure one medium-sized apple per serving.) Stuff with a layer of **Bread Crumbs,** sprinkle with **Maple Sugar** or **Brown Sugar** and **Cinnamon** and dot generously with **Butter.** Repeat layers till full. Top with sweetened **Applesauce.** Bake at 350° F. for 40 minutes. Serve with a **Brandy Hard Sauce.** (See next recipe.)

HARD SAUCE

Cream together ½ cup of **Butter** and 1 cup of **Confectioner's Sugar,** adding the sugar a little at a time and beating until the mixture is very smooth and light. Flavor to taste with **Cognac,** any **Liqueur, Vanilla, Orange Juice** and a little grated **Orange Rind,** finely chopped **Ginger** or any other flavoring that you choose.

hot and fragrant
APPLE CRUNCH

Peel and core 4 large tart **Apples.** Cut them in thin slices and place half of them in the bottom of a well-greased, shallow baking dish or casserole. Sprinkle with ¼ cup **Granulated Sugar** and add the remaining apples.

Now combine 1 cup **Light Brown Sugar** with 1 cup **Sifted Flour** and 1 cup finely chopped **Pecans.** Cream ½ cup **Butter** and work in the flour mixture gradually, with ½ teaspoon **Cinnamon.** When well blended, spread it over the apples, pressing the edges down firmly. Slit the surface two or three times and bake 50 minutes at 350° F. Serve it with **Whipped Cream** or **Heavy Cream.** It is best when straight from the oven. Serves 8.

how to be popular
APPLES AU RHUM

Peel, core and cut in half 4 large tart **Apples.** Place them cut side up in a casserole.

Blend together over low heat to make a syrup 4 tablespoons **Peach Jam** or **Preserve,** the juice and grated rind of 1 **Orange,** ½ cup **Water** and ½ cup **Sugar.** As soon as thickened, remove from flame and add 3 tablespoons **Rum.** Pour over apples and bake at 350° F. for 30 minutes. Serve cold with **Whipped Cream.** Serves 8.

everybody's favorite
BAKED APPLES

Core as many **Apples** as you'll need for servings and pare them down around the top about an inch. Place them in a casserole or baking dish with ½ inch of **Water.** Fill each one of the apples with **Sugar** or sugar and **Cinnamon** mixed—about 2 tablespoons to each apple. Dot generously with **Butter** and bake 30 to 40 minutes at 350° F., basting often with the syrup in the dish. When done they should be lightly glazed. Serve them either hot or cold with **Heavy Cream, Whipped Cream** or **Sour Cream.**

Variations

1. Fill the centers with a mixture of **Plumped Raisins** (ones soaked to fullness), chopped **Nuts** and **Honey.** Spread the tops of the apples with additional honey and baste with the juices in the pan.

2. Use a combination of **Brown Sugar** and chopped **Walnuts.**

3. Add a tablespoon or so of grated **Orange Rind** to the sugar; dot with butter and baste with **Orange Juice.**

4. Fill the centers with butter and **Brown Sugar**

APPLE KITCHEN

Baked apple, sugared, cinnamoned and served with cream, is an old unbeatable favorite.

creamed together. Baste with **Applejack** added to the pan juice.

5. Fill the apples with a mixture of stale **Cake Crumbs, Raisins** and a little sugar moistened with melted butter. Sprinkle additional crumbs over the tops and bake as above.

fancy fruit
BANANA PUDDING

Peel and mash 12 **Ripe Bananas.** Combine the pulp with 2 beaten **Eggs,** ¼ pound melted **Butter,** 2 tablespoons **Rum** and **Nutmeg** and **Sugar** to taste.

Sift ½ cup **Flour** with 2 tablespoons **Baking Powder.** Blend with the banana mixture and pour into a buttered casserole. Bake at 400° F. until the mixture is bubbly, then reduce heat to 275° F. and continue cooking till a silver knife, when inserted, comes out clean. Cool before serving with **Whipped Cream** or very **Heavy Cream.** Serves 6.

after a heavy meal
LEMON RICE PUDDING

Boil ½ cup **Raw Rice** in 1 quart **Milk** until it is soft. While still hot—but not cooking—add 3 beaten **Egg Yolks,** 1 tablespoon **Butter,** 4 tablespoons **Sugar,** the grated rind and the juice of 1½ **Lemons,** and ¼ teaspoon **Salt.** Return to very low heat and let thicken, stirring constantly.

Pour into a casserole. Top with a meringue of 3 beaten **Egg Whites** to which 6 tablespoons sugar and juice of ½ lemon have been gently folded in. Brown in a slow oven and then let cool. The pudding thickens as it gets cooler. Serves 6.

holiday idea
SWEET POTATO PUDDING

Mix together 2½ cups of mashed, cooked **Yams** with 1 cup of **Light Brown Sugar;** beat till smooth. Add 1 tablespoon **Molasses,** 1 teaspoon ground **Cinnamon,** 1 teaspoon ground **Ginger,** ¼ teaspoon grated **Nutmeg,** ½ teaspoon **Salt,** 2 tablespoons melted **Butter,** 3 **Beaten Eggs** and the finely shredded peel of half a **Tangerine.** Blend thoroughly and turn into a buttered casserole. Bake at 350° F. 1 hour until firm.

Remove from oven and sprinkle with 2 or 3 tablespoons of **Curacao** or **Cointreau.** Let stand about 15 minutes and serve with **Heavy Cream.** If the yams are not very sweet, add **White Sugar** to taste. Serves 6.

Try this with turkey or duck.

family standby
BREAD PUDDING

Add 2 cups of cubed soft **Bread** to 1 quart scalded **Milk.** Set it aside and let the bread soak 15 minutes. Beat 2 **Eggs** slightly and add ⅓ cup **Sugar** and ½ teaspoon **Salt.** When well blended, combine with the bread mixture and stir in ¼ cup melted **Butter,** 1 tablespoon grated **Lemon Peel** and **Vanilla** to taste. Pour into a greased baking dish, place in a pan of warm water and bake 1 hour and 15 minutes at 350° F. When done, a silver knife when inserted will come out clean. Serves 6.

real flavor
ORANGE BREAD PUDDING

Remove the crusts from 7 slices of **Bread. Butter** the slices generously, break them into pieces and place in a greased 8-inch casserole. Sprinkle them with 1 tablespoon grated **Orange** rind and the grated rind of 1 **Lemon.** Beat 4 **Eggs** with ½ cup **Sugar.** Add 2 cups **Orange Juice** (the juice of 1 **Lemon** should be part of the 2 cups) and beat again. Pour over the bread and let stand an hour. Bake at 325°F. for 40 minutes. Serve with **Brandy Sauce** (see next recipe). Serves 6.

BRANDY SAUCE

Bring 1 cup **Cream** to a boil and place over hot water, not boiling; add ½ cup **Butter.** Beat 4 **Egg Yolks** until lemon-colored. Gradually pour in 1 cup **Sugar** and beat again. Combine with hot cream and butter. Let thicken over low heat, stirring constantly. Just before serving add cognac (or bourbon) to taste.

rich and heady
PEACH COBBLER

Line a well-buttered casserole with a **Rich Biscuit Dough.** Fill with sliced **Peaches** (1 peach for each serving) almost to the top, sprinkling the layers with **Sugar** and dotting them with **Butter.** Dribble on 3 or 4 tablespoons **Rum.** Top with more biscuit dough and brush with melted butter. Prick in several places with a fork and bake 25 minutes at 375° F. Serve with a **Hard Sauce** (see next recipe).

HARD SAUCE

Cream together ½ cup of **Butter** and 1 cup of **Confectioner's Sugar,** adding the sugar a little at a time and beating until the mixture is very smooth and light. Flavor to taste with any one of these: **Cognac,** any **Liqueur, Vanilla, Orange Juice** and a little grated **Orange Rind,** finely chopped **Ginger** or any other flavoring that you choose.

very neat treat

CHILLED CUSTARD

Scald 1 pint **Heavy Cream** in top of double boiler. Beat 6 **Egg Yolks** until light and foamy. Add ¼ teaspoon **Salt** and ¼ cup **Granulated Sugar** and beat until sugar is dissolved. Pour hot cream slowly over eggs and blend well. Return to double boiler and continue cooking over hot, not boiling water. Stir continuously until the mixture coats the spoon. Remove from heat and stir in 1 teaspoon **Vanilla**.

Pour into a shallow, very heatproof casserole. Place, uncovered, in the refrigerator and chill overnight or at least 6 hours.

Before serving, remove from refrigerator and sprinkle the top with 1 cup **Light Brown Sugar**. Place immediately under broiler, 6 inches from flame, and broil until sugar melts. Don't let it burn. Return to refrigerator to let crust harden and leave until serving. Serves 6 to 8.

10

HOW TO IMPROVISE

I've been cooking for fun and for profit a great many years now and I've written more than a few books on the subject. But it was just the other day that a friend of mine made a very sensible suggestion to me.

"Why is it," he asked, "that you people who write cookbooks always tell the reader to do this or that exactly thus and so and no other way? You know as well as I do that any cook worth his salt will always make somes change or other, either because of a personal prejudice or because some of the ingredients just aren't handy. And we all like to experiment!"

I began to think about that and I couldn't help seeing some justice in his complaint. One of the reasons for this is that the people who make a business out of cooking and writing about it usually have experimented for years and when they get a dish just exactly the way they like it, they figure this is the way it should be, and no back talk about it.

On the other hand, what is a cook without an independent imagination? So—I am going to break one of the rules of the trade here. I'm going to tell you now some of the secrets of improvisation. Just remember— it is always a good idea to follow the directions exactly the first time you try a recipe. But from then on, you're on your own.

If a recipe calls for liquid or stock, use any broths you may have on hand: meat broth; chicken or game stock; vegetable broths left over from cooking vegetables; tomato juice; thinned-down tomato purée or tomato sauce; any other vegetable juices; or a combination of any of these.

Wines and liquors used as part of the liquid add flavor to many dishes, particularly those using meats or fowl. If the basic food in the casserole is delicately flavored, however, go easy on wine or liquor or you may drown all other taste. And remember, just because a little wine is good in a dish, a great deal will not necessarily be better.

Many meats go well with fruit juices. Let your taste buds be your guide in using such juices.

When fresh tomatoes are in season and reasonable in price, use them in recipes calling for tomato sauce. Make a sauce of them in the following way: Peel, seed and chop three or four medium tomatoes and cook them slowly in four to six tablespoons of butter or oil. Add a little salt and a pinch or so of basil. Use fresh basil leaves, if they are available. When the tomatoes have cooked down to a smooth paste, put them through a sieve.

Tomato purée, diluted with a little tomato juice or red wine, makes an excellent liquid for many casseroles. If you are using canned tomato sauce as an added dressing to serve with some meat or vegetable dish, add a little sugar, salt, freshly ground black pepper and butter to it while it is heating. Taste for seasoning.

In changing ingredients in the meat or fish category, a simple rule to follow is to substitute something similar. If the casserole calls for a smoked meat, try to substitute some other variety of smoked meat, for generally the smoky flavor is the taste that should be retained in these dishes. If the meat is delicately flavored, use something equally delicate in its place. If it is heavy and rich, select a rich substitute.

As for fish, substitute one shellfish for another—a light fish for one that is delicate, a meaty fish for one that is heavy. Of course, there are many exceptions to this general rule, but the exceptions must be discovered by experimentation. That is where your own imagination can take the lead.

With vegetables as with meats, try to substitute a similar item. For example, many recipes call for shallots. The shallot is a small reddish bulb of the onion family. In many parts of the country it is not available. In some areas, such as New Orleans, the scallion or small green onion is called shallot. You may substitute green onions or any other member of the onion family, though the flavor will not be exactly duplicated.

Seasonings, herbs and spices are items to be handled with great discrimination. They can make or ruin a dish, and their overuse, along with overcooking, is one of the great faults of beginners. Be cautious with herbs. Better too little than too much. Use bay leaf with discreation; its flavor can be overpowering. Too much thyme gives a bitter tang. Many people find sage indigestible or just plain dislike it. It is better to omit it entirely, but if you must use it, use it sparingly. Rosemary is another herb that some people try to avoid. You can use a little oregano or summer savory instead. But be careful with oregano, for it has a bold flavor. It is often better combined with other herbs. There is no substitute for tarragon, and this herb is something every cook should have on hand.

As for the old stand-bys—salt and pepper—they, too, need special attention from the cook. Strangely enough, most people under-salt. Taste if you are not sure. I find the coarse salt, either Malden salt or Kosher, the best. As for pepper, always use freshly ground black pepper. It alone has the full spicy tang pepper should have. Buy a pepper mill; it's a life-long investment in good food, so don't balk at the price.

Two delicious seasonings often used too sparingly by the cook are curry and chili. Be brave. These are both hot, to be sure, but they are meant to be. You can't get the full flavor of either unless you use enough to make their taste pronounced. If some of your family or guests cannot stand hot food, make the main dish with a mild amount of the seasoning, and serve an extra bowl of very hot curry sauce or chili sauce alongside.

The substitution of spices in desserts is up to the individual taste. With some people cinnamon is the favorite. Others prefer nutmeg. Some have a passion for ginger or cloves. My only suggestion: Try a variety.

Remember, however, spices are included in entrées for their specific tang. For example, many meat dishes call for a clove or two or an onion stuck with one or two cloves. These are important. A word of warning: When a spice is used in a meat dish, use it sparingly. The flavor should not be noticeable. One or two cloves is enough. A tiny amount of ginger in recipes calling for that flavor is ample. Unlike desserts, meat dishes need spice to point up another flavor, not to be dominant.

Saffron is an odd flavoring that can provide just the right touch, if used carefully. A tiny pinch goes a long way. Too much will make the dish bitter.

Always use the best available, even if it costs a little more. Artificial vanilla is a poor money-saver. It tastes artificial. Use genuine vanilla syrup or, better yet, a vanilla bean. Buy the bean, put it in a jar and fill the jar with sugar. This sugar can be used in desserts calling for vanilla flavor. Replace the sugar as you use it. You can also use small pieces of vanilla bean in sugar syrup for poaching fruit.

Mustard is another item on which you should not try to save pennies. Most inexpensive bottled mustard put up in this country is much too bland to be interesting. There are one or two American bottled mustards (for example, Gulden's) that are good. For the most part, the imports are by far the best. German and Dutch mustards are good, as are the mustards from Dijon, France, made with white wine and seasonings. You can make an excellent mustard yourself by mixing dry mustard with a little vinegar or white wine. This is very hot and should be used gently. Make it fresh each time you need it, for it dries out quickly. You might try rubbing it on chicken or beef before braising. It imparts a wonderful pungent taste.

Many a cook attains outstanding results by adding a "dash of this" or a "pinch of that." This ability is something that comes with long experience, self-confidence and, most important, a taste imagination. That is, the flair for imagining what two flavors will taste like together. If you want to experiment, begin on yourself, not on your family or guests. After you are sure of the results and satisfied with them, then is the time to stake your reputation on your own creation.

The most important thing is your attitude toward preparing a meal. Relax and enjoy cooking it, and then enjoy eating it, savoring each mouthful and appreciating each new flavor. You will find that, in no time at all, the ideas for creating your own specialties will clamor for expression.

11

WHAT GOES WITH WHAT

In the opening section of the main dishes, I promised you an entire chapter on suggested accompaniments besides my individual recommendations following the recipes. Here they are, for your personal selection. I'm sure that on these next few pages you'll be able to find something new and exciting to add to your repertoire. Naturally, these dishes can be used with a wide variety of meals besides those that come from the casserole, but they are all picked primarily because they fit into the casserole scheme for one reason or another. Help yourself.

FOR MEAT DISHES

hot vegetables

1. Sauté French-cut string beans in olive oil with garlic. Cover them and steam them in the oil for about ten minutes, or until just barely cooked through. Season to taste with salt and pepper.

2. Steam tiny peas under damp lettuce leaves, and flavor with a little onion and ham.

3. Cook a head of cauliflower until just tender. Serve with almonds sautéed in butter until lightly browned.

4. Sauté strips of green pepper in olive oil with a touch of garlic and a dash of wine vinegar.

5. Sauté, in butter, raw corn cut off the cob, with the addition of a few strips of green pepper, if you like.

6. Cook globe artichokes and serve with Hollandaise sauce.

7. Braise endive.

8. Braise celery.

9. Cook asparagus until just barely done and serve with butter or Hollandaise sauce.

10. Sauté green onions in butter, then cover and steam until just tender.

11. Steam sliced Spanish onions in butter and sprinkle with sharp grated cheese just before removing from the stove.

12. Cook white beans in bouillon and a seasoning of garlic, salt and pepper.

cold vegetables

1. Slice raw cauliflower paper-thin and treat like cole slaw.

2. Grate raw corn and mix it with sour cream or whipped cream.

3. Cabbage slaw.

4. Cold cooked asparagus served with mayonnaise and garnished with capers and chopped green onions.

5. Romaine leaves with dunk sauce.

6. Endive with dunk sauce.

7. Green onions.

8. Grated raw celery root mixed with a mustard-flavored mayonnaise.

9. Various kinds of pickles.

FOR FISH DISHES

hot vegetables

Thinly sliced celery sautéed quickly in butter with salt, pepper and tarragon. It should still be crisp and green when served.

cold vegetables

1. Cole slaw with sour cream dressing.
2. Cucumber salad with sour cream and fresh dill.
3. Shredded cucumbers with equal amounts of sour cream and mayonnaise, flavored with onion and fresh dill.
4. Thinly sliced tomatoes with an herb dressing. Use basil, parsley or rosemary.
5. Fingers of endive with salt and pepper.
6. Celery, radishes, green onions, Italian celery or fenel with salt and pepper.

SALAD SUGGESTIONS

1. Serve ice cold artichoke hearts with a rich mayonnaise, seasoned with chopped onion or scallions.
2. Paper-thin slices of oranges and onions are good with rosemary and lemon juice. Olive oil is optional.
3. Don't forget sliced pickled beets. Or beets and onions sliced together with a well-seasoned French dressing.
4. Have well-chopped beets sometime, seasoned with the least bit of good vinegar. Cover them with mayonnaise and top with sieved hard-boiled eggs.
5. Break hearts of romaine in bite-sized pieces and toss with crumbled crisp bacon. Add chopped onion and pour over all the hot bacon fat. Add a bit of red wine vinegar. Toss again and serve hot.

6. Shredded raw celery root is delicious with mayonnaise and mustard added to it. And thin slivers of celery are also excellent when served in this same manner.

7. Try shredded celery with a dressing of sour cream and plenty of fresh dill.

8. For a different and delicious vegetable salad, have cold cooked fresh peas with mayonnaise and shredded lettuce.

9. That old stand-by, grapefruit with avocado slices, dressed with oil and lemon juice, is as good as they come. And one of my favorites is a salad of sliced avocados with chopped green onions and ripe olives, with the same dressing.

10. Make a fine oil dressing with your best vinegar and add it to chopped ripe olives and onion. Pour this generously over cold tender cooked string beans.

11. Find some black radishes if you can. Grate them and serve with a mustard mayonnaise.

12. Tender Boston lettuce leaves can steal the show with chopped hard-boiled egg, garlic croutons and a delicious oil and lemon juice dressing sprinkled over the top.

13. White beans with chopped onion and tomato and a well-seasoned French dressing, with a green of your choice, may be served as an hors d'oeuvre or a salad, or as an extra dish for that big buffet you have been planning.

14. Try a potato salad with slivers of celery and green onion, a quantity of chopped parsley and an oil-lemon juice dressing.

15. Season a mayonnaise well with tomato sauce and mustard. Serve with cold cooked rice which you have tossed with a sprinkling of curry powder, chopped onion, chopped tomatoes and a touch of fresh parsley and rosemary.

16. Crisp raw vegetables are good at almost any meal, either with a dunk sauce or just plain salt and pepper.

17. For a change, try cold cooked sauerkraut with plenty of chopped onion, freshly and coarsely ground black pepper and a pungent French dressing.

18. And don't forget such faithful old stand-bys as sliced cucumbers, onion rings, sliced tomatoes with fresh basil, sour pickles, dill pickles (made with real dill), pickled walnuts, pickled mushrooms and all the vast and wonderful olive family.